Wine

A WOMAN'S GUIDE

Kitty Johnson

BANTAM PRESS

LONDON · NEW YORK · TORONTO · SYDNEY · AUCKLAND

TRANSWORLD PUBLISHERS
61–63 Uxbridge Road, London W5 5SA
a division of The Random House Group Ltd

RANDOM HOUSE AUSTRALIA (PTY) LTD
20 Alfred Street, Milsons Point, Sydney,
New South Wales 2061, Australia

RANDOM HOUSE NEW ZEALAND LTD
18 Poland Road, Glenfield, Auckland 10, New Zealand

RANDOM HOUSE SOUTH AFRICA (PTY) LTD
Endulini, 5a Jubilee Road, Parktown 2193, South Africa

Published 2003 by Bantam Press
a division of Transworld Publishers

Designed and typeset by Julia Lloyd

A catalogue record for this book is available from the British Library.
ISBN 0593 049934

Printed in Italy.

1 3 5 7 9 10 8 6 4 2

Inspired by men, dedicated to women

I may not here omit these two plagues, and common dotages of human kind, wine and women, which have infatuated and besotted myriads of people. They go commonly together.

ROBERT BURTON, 1577–1640

There is not the hundredth part of the wine consumed in this kingdom that there ought to be. Our foggy climate wants help.

JANE AUSTEN, 1775–1817, *NORTHANGER ABBEY*

Contents

Acknowledgements

A HUGE THANK-YOU TO MY BROTHER, RED, FOR PLANTING THE idea in my head in the first place; my father, Hugh, for sharing his passion for the subject and introducing me to the (wine) bottle at such a tender age; and my loving and loyal husband, Chris, for his unending patience and support. Thanks also to the girls in my family, all my fabulous friends, Robert Joseph – a great teacher, my agent Araminta Whitley and her assistant Celia Hayley, to Sally Gaminara for her guidance, Mari Roberts for her skilful 'waffle' cropping and everybody else involved at Transworld Publishers. Thanks also to my invaluable researchers, Rowan Rose Boyson and Mark and Fiona Taylor. Thanks to all the contributors: Merrilees Parker for her food tips; Nico Thiriot of Sainsbury's Calais; Sarah Kemp at *Decanter* magazine; Nicky Forrest at Phipps PR; Gaby Allen at Carpe Diem Communications; Sue Harris at Westbury Communications; Lindsay Talas at Tesco; Jane Masters MW at Marks and Spencer; Amanda Skinner, Managing Director of John Armit Wines; Kate Thal, Wine Consultant; Emma Wellings at Emma Wellings PR; Brookes and Vernon; Bass Leisure Retail; Youngs Brewery, and James Aufenast of *Hot* magazine. And to whoever is reading this now, thank you for picking it up.

Introduction

CAST YOUR MIND BACK TO THE NEOLITHIC PERIOD, THE LATE Stone Age, somewhere between about 8000 and 4000 BC. For those of you with hazy recollections of what you were up to last Friday night, this could be stretching it a bit. Although first-hand confirmation is hard to come by, experts and scholars suggest it was a *woman*, somewhere in the Middle East, who first encountered fermented grapes (left lying about in a sun trap, perhaps). She drank the juice they provided and was delighted to find it had rather a giddying effect.

Today, women buy more wine than men do, and they drink more wine than any other alcohol. It's not a luxury or an occasional treat, it's part of life. For most of the intervening millennia, however, the picture has looked rather different. Consumption was dictated by men, who decided that 'respectable' women couldn't drink, and that 'loose' women could, perhaps, but it would affect their behaviour far more deleteriously than it did any man. Pliny the Elder put it plainly: 'It is not permitted to women at Rome to drink wine.' Lower-class women – prostitutes, musicians and dancers – were allowed to drink quite freely when invited as accessories to a *symposion* in Greece or a *convivium* in

Rome (formalized, male-led, after-meal gatherings at private homes), and the same women were required to pick up the 'we-can-handle-our-wine-thanks-very-much' men from the floor at the end of the night. Roman taverns, *popinae*, were often managed by women, who offered food, drink and sex to their male customers: multi-tasking prototypes.

This attitude towards women and wine went against the grain, or grape, as far as religion was concerned. Many early deities linked to wine were female. Take Gestin, the Sumerian goddess of the vine, or the demi-god Danel's daughter, who helped cultivate vines in Syria. The Egyptian snake-goddess Renen-utet was present at all the vintages. Then, of course, there were the Maenads, or Bacchae – Greek women who were encouraged to find liberation from controlling spouses and to let their hair down, rip apart animals and drink wine and blood during the winter worship of Dionysus, the god of wine. But in typical Greek society, men's control of women was commonplace and, according to Plutarch, could range from prohibition on eating lettuce-hearts to wholesale bans on walking at large in order to avoid being stolen by pirates.

As wine continued to play its part in both religious and secular society throughout the Middle Ages, its suitability for women remained an issue. 'A drunk woman is not the mistress of her body,' declared a sixteenth-century proverb. Women found in pubs and bars in the eighteenth century were considered no better than ladies of the night. So too in the nineteenth century, when decent Victorian women stayed at home and men went to pubs to get away from them. Any drinking women did do was done behind closed doors. Things didn't start to pick up for us until after World War Two, and for a time even then if you were in a pub unaccompanied by a man it was assumed you were offering your services – and not as a cleaning lady.

A glorious exception, a tiny glimpse of greater possibilities, was Champagne. Even in the nineteenth century it was considered a drink for almost any occasion (at least within the middle and aristocratic classes) and one that women could also enjoy. Father-to-son inheritance was the norm in Europe's wine industry – look at the number of *père et fils* (father and son) joint-venture French wines on our off-licence shelves even today – but it was the nineteenth-century widow Veuve Clicquot, submerging herself in the family business to ease her grief, whose development of an efficient means to expel the yeasty sediment from bottles of bubbly (*remuage*), and whose opening up of new export channels, helped make Champagne the talked-about marvel it is today. Her Champagne pops up on wine-shop shelves all around the country and her famous orange-label brand still fizzes at social events. Also in the nineteenth century, Jeanne Alexandrine Louise Pommery built up the House of Pommery to unpredicted heights after the death of her founder-husband. Fabulous fizzy had elite female clients then just as it does today – film-stars and supermodels bathe in it regularly, so I am told.

Among today's top women is Baroness Philippine de Rothschild of the Bordeaux dynasty, who took over from her father at Mouton-Rothschild in 1988. With one of the world's most expensive wines – first-growth Château Mouton-Rothschild – and one of the world's biggest brands, Moûton-Cadet, on the family CV, she went on to expand the portfolio further, incorporating Vin de Pays wines (labelled with the grape variety – a French revolution) and setting up joint ventures overseas. No mean feat.

In the last twenty to thirty years, an increasing number of women around the world have chosen to make wine their career, often by studying viticulture and oenology (the study of wine) at one of the major institutes or universities: Bordeaux in France, Geisenheim in

Germany, Davis in California or Roseworthy in Australia. It is not surprising to see women working among the vines of the New World wine regions, where the industries have accelerated in the last twenty years to compete with global demand. Well-trained and knowledgeable women winemakers pop up from the Andes to the Outback, in places where innovation and experimentation across the trade have meant that women in responsible roles are less likely to be the subject of curiosity or interrogation.

Let us not forget the wine writers, of course. Jancis Robinson was the first non-wine-trade Master of Wine in this country, and is a highly successful author and broadcaster. Then there's Jilly Goolden, who has slurped on screen, to the delight and occasional irritation of many a TV viewer, accompanied by her panoply of flavour adjectives. The national papers are filled with columns from women writers, all of whom have had influence on female acceptance into the ram-filled fold.

It would be unrealistic of me to suggest that the scene is entirely rosy for us now. Men still hold more of the cards. The wine trade, by its closed and clubby nature, has evolved towards sexual equality more slowly than other industries. It appeals to the train-spotting gene in men. The science of wine satisfies blokes who spend hours poring over car manuals, while their competitive gene is exercised by big-bucks decision-making for leading brands. But as more and more women are getting their hands wine-stained in fermentation tanks, or organizing the quick shipping of 30,000 wine cases to an impatient supermarket, we are also bringing with us different concerns. Women have a more relaxed approach to communicating about wine, which removes the competitive edge so many consumers find off-putting. Men come to the tasting arena with stronger preconceptions, often bogged down by the traditionalism and mystique of wine. Women are more open-minded, and by judging a wine on its own merit are in some ways more honest as well. And we really do have a higher number of receptors on our tongues, which makes us the superior tasters. Sorry, lads.

In the promotion and marketing of wine, certainly in Britain, women have got their high heels firmly in the door. Many of the PR companies that deal with wine, and indeed food, are made up of women. Women tend to have considerable skills in the networking and socializing element of the wine industry, and far less interest in boasting about the size of their cellar.

So who should know best what women want from wine than women themselves? It's time to take decision-making into our own hands, even if it's no more momentous than choosing just the right bottle of wine from your local off-licence to have with dinner tonight. Come with me on this journey through the world of wine and learn to understand it and to define your own tastes. You need never be baffled by a wine list or boggled by wine-shop shelves or intimidated by anyone else's knowledge again.

CHAPTER ONE

A Question of Style

LIFE ITSELF, IT SEEMS, IS A GOOD ENOUGH EXCUSE TO OPEN A bottle of wine these days. We no longer consider it a great luxury or a treat – although we might if we were to indulge in something bank-breakingly expensive. Even sparkling wine is rarely saved for a special occasion. We hardly think twice about having a bottle of bubbly in the bath on a Friday night to smooth away the worries of a working week or to limber up before a night out on the tiles. For many of us, wine is part of everyday life.

So, we drink wine in the bathroom, in the kitchen, in the sitting room and sometimes in bed. We drink it in pubs (without shame), in wine bars, clubs, restaurants, cafés, the theatre, the opera and even in certain cinemas. We drink it by the glass, by the bottle, out of boxes or out of cans. We drink it before, during and after a meal, and sometimes we drink it by itself. We drink wine with other women, with men and on our own. We sometimes drink at lunchtime and in the early evening, and we often drink at night. Friday and Saturday nights are the best lubricated but a glass or two on a working-week night is not a sinful thought or a scandalous act.

Many of us are enjoying an extended youth. We are waiting longer to get married and have kids (or even putting this off altogether!). Where once we would have been washing non-disposable nappies, now we are pursuing a career and enjoying a disposable income. And this means we are going out, letting our hair down, enjoying a glass or two of wine and unwinding after a stressful day.

The places allocated to de-stressing and hair unpinning are increasingly female-friendly. The dingy, smoky, 'dirty old men collapsed on bar stools' pubs of the past have been replaced by glass-fronted, lighter, airier, better located wine bars with wine that is, at last, often actually drinkable and certainly comes in ever greater variety.

Wine choosing is easier for us than it is for the instinctively competitive male. We feel less pressure when we undergo the saturated-with-options selection process. For us, the things that make a 'right' wine decision are what it tastes like, its price and what the bottle looks like. For men, 'How will my choice play to the crowd here?' often comes before 'Will I like this?'

Just as a man spends two hours driving round in circles before finally admitting to being lost and even then won't ask for directions, neither will he admit to needing advice on wine choice. Men have been given authority in and command of the subject of wine, rightly or wrongly, since its discovery way back when. Women, on the other hand, have less expected of them in their relationship with wine, and therefore less to lose. We don't mind asking for advice and accepting suggestions, and we are happy to choose wine on the most obvious – and valid – basis of all: because we like the taste.

'A glass of white wine for the lady'

We do have our sticking points, of course. Sixty per cent of us prefer white wine to red. And red is indeed a tougher colour to conquer. To begin with, the tannins can be a bit of a mouthful. Tannins are the mouth-drying and teeth-staining components (imagine, if you dare, my unsightly, witch-like black teeth after a tasting of fifty-plus young, tannic reds from Bordeaux), which are similarly found in tea – picture the brown tidemark in a poorly washed tea mug. They come from the skins, pips and stalks of red grapes, which are also where red wine gets its colour, in particular from the skins: open up a red grape and you will see that the flesh inside, which provides the juice, is virtually colourless. Tannins also act as a preservative, enabling red wines to age for longer. The good news is that tannins soften as a wine gets older, so if you find younger reds, like younger men, too hard to handle (think Robbie Williams), try drinking more mature wines with gentler tannins but more complexity (more Sean Connery) or soft, low-tannin red wine varieties (funny, cuddly creatures like John Candy or Timothy Spall), such as Merlot, Gamay (in Beaujolais), Pinot Noir or Tempranillo (in Rioja). The other good news for the more senior among us is that we begin to lose our sensitivity to bitter substances after menopause. Tannins taste bitter, so this character in wine will bother us less by then.

Another reason for the red resistance is that red wines are responsible for more allergic responses than white. Among these reactions are headaches, migraines, unsightly red rashes that spread across your face and neck (the technical term is vasodilation), and even aggravated eczema and asthma. Red wines have also been blamed for causing a more intense hangover hell than white. The cause? A higher level of complex organic chemical compounds in red wine (found in the flavour- and colour-providing grape skins), thought to include allergy-triggering histamines.

I didn't like red wine at all until I was about twenty-two (along with olives and hot spicy food), which corresponds nicely with recent findings that show how younger or less experienced wine consumers drink white wine exclusively, whereas those with a broader wine knowledge and more drinking years behind them are more likely to drink both. I still don't like marzipan or kidneys, but that's another story.

By their mid-twenties most women are coming round to reds. Not only do the high levels of acidity in white wine often wreak havoc on more sensitive digestive systems (as does sparkling wine, many women find) but red wine also comes up trumps on health benefits too. I go into the issue of health in more detail later in the book. For now, let's get down to business.

Wine styles

Whoever we are, whoever we're with, whatever the time, the occasion, the weather, the place, the mood, there is a wine style to suit. That, to me, is one of the greatest wonders of wine.

The many and magnificent winemaking countries of the world are capable of producing wines of immense variety in colour, flavour and even texture. We can begin to find our way around by mapping these wines according to style. The factors influencing styles are manifold, but principally they are these: the type of grape, the climate in which it is grown, and how, once fermented into an alcoholic liquid, the wine is nurtured into adulthood, both in the winery and then in the bottle.

Whites

Zingy and Citrussy

These wines are typically made with minimal intervention along the way. They are made from grapes that are happier in cooler climates and are picked fairly young, still brimming with acidity. The resulting wine spends only a short time (a couple of months) in stainless-steel tanks before being bottled and shipped out, as foot-loose, fancy-free and fresh-faced as possible. These are young wines to be drunk and enjoyed in their youth; they have little ageing potential.

Smell/taste: lemons and limes, grass, gooseberry, pear drops, green apples
Colour: very pale, almost watery white
Look for: Sancerre, Pouilly-Fumé and other European Sauvignon Blancs, Pinot Grigio, Orvieto, Verdicchio and other light, northern Italian whites, Muscadet from the Loire, Vinho Verde from Portugal, young unoaked Semillon, Colombard

Fitting them into your lifestyle

These light, fresh styles don't demand too much of those who indulge in them. They are warm-weather wines and need to be drunk well chilled (8–12°C). They are out-doorsy drinks for picnics in the park, for summery lunches when you wish to stay reasonably in charge of your faculties, or for light aperitifs at dusk. Their typically moderate alcohol levels (between 11.5 and 13 per cent) make them appropriate for daytime. Their naturally high acidity makes them mouth-watering and moreish, setting you up well for continued drinking or whetting your appetite before a meal. These wines are not meant for rich, heavy foods. Their delicacy is better suited to fish, seafood, salads or nibbles – the way they have always been enjoyed in their lands of origin.

Neutral and Smooth

Made in a similar way to the *zingy and citrussy* style, these wines have a little more concentration of flavour. They might spend longer developing flavour in stainless-steel tanks, and they might also undergo either or both of two possible processes that soften and enrich them: malolactic fermentation (the conversion of sharp malic acid to creamy lactic acid), or lees contact (contact with dead post-ferment yeast cells). The resulting wines are smooth movers, still with a freshness of flavour but not quite so tongue prickly as the zingers. Made well, these wines have a greater propensity to age.

Smell/taste: honey, almonds, stones, wet wool, pears, peaches; at best faintly aromatic
Colour: pale yellow
Look for: Gavi and good Soave from Italy, Pinot Blanc from Alsace or the United States, Chablis from Burgundy, Chenin Blanc from Vouvray or, slightly less smooth, from South Africa

Fitting them into your lifestyle

These elegant but rounded wines combine finesse with mouth-filling flavour. The best are worth taking your time over or even laying down in the cellar for a few years to reap the rewards of their development in the bottle. They are also best at lower temperatures, about the same as *zingy and citrussy*, if not a degree or two warmer. These wines serve a similar purpose: al fresco fun, although they can handle tastier foods better. They would have no trouble taking on a chicken dish or even a stir-fry. Relaxing wines to smooth out the creases of your day.

Rich and Nutty

These wines have either been made with oak or have matured in the bottle. The best are made with grapes that have reached ripeness but still have life-giving acidity. After malolactic fermentation, lees contact and/or oak exposure, the resulting wines will be rich and complex with different layers and dimensions of flavour. These wines, like Joan Collins, are built to last and often look even better with age.

Smell/taste: honey, nuts, cream, toast, lime, apricots, baked apples, spices

Colour: pale gold
Look for: oaked Graves or Pessac-Leognan (Bordeaux), mature New World Semillon, Burgundy, Marsanne from Australia

Fitting them into your lifestyle

These monsters have loads of life and aren't designed for emergency gulping. Cracking open one of the prime examples is an excuse for a party in itself. The best will be richly concentrated and shown off at their optimum if not too overly chilled (10–13°C; a little warmer for the bigger Burgundies at 13–15°C). These are foodie wines for lunch or dinner parties when you are serving fish, chicken or pasta. They are in-law impressors or colleague wow-ers. They are all-year-rounders as well, just as comfily quaffed at the Christmas table as they would be sipped on a summer's lawn.

Toasty and Buttery

Such wines have spent a long time in oak, maybe even a couple of years. They have probably been fermented in oak barrels and certainly matured in them afterwards. To a certain extent naturally oxidized, they will have developed complex flavours as well as taken on the character of the oak.

Smell/taste: toast, butter, honey, vanilla, spice, baked or dried fruit, pineapples, bananas
Colour: rich and golden
Look for: oaked Semillon, white Rioja, oaked Chardonnay from anywhere but Burgundy, Roussanne from Australia

Fitting them into your lifestyle

Stand back for some of the weightiest white wines in the world, where oak influence is the overwhelming message for the mouth. These wines are hugely rich in hot-buttered-toast flavour and probably carry a fair whack of sweetness-suggesting alcohol too. To pull back on the oak impact, they are best served that little bit warmer than other whites too (13–15°C). All-weather-friendly and food-needy, fussy only in that they can act as a smothering blanket over more delicately flavoured ingredients. These are evening wines, dinner-party perfect, as well as being the ultimate complement to the good old Sunday roast. They are slow sippers-and-savourers, not gulping material. Stand up slowly after a few...

Spicy and Aromatic

Often made without too much intervention in the winery (i.e. oak) so as to maintain their unique, often aromatic, characterful ways, these are quirky wines. They are distinctive and easily recognizable. They may be fresh and lively or mature and more developed but either way they are a simple reflection of the character of the grape.

Smell/taste: flowers, spices, grapes, lime, lychees, tropical fruit, passionfruit, honey, apricots and green peppers (depending on the different varietals)
Colour: fairly pale (this may also vary according to the different varietals)
Look for: Riesling, Rhône whites (Viognier), Albariño from Spain, Torrontes from Argentina, Muscat (Moscatel), Alsace and New World Pinot Gris, Gewürztraminer, New World Sauvignon Blanc, Verdelho

Fitting them into your lifestyle

With some of these wines it's hard to know whether to drink them, spray them behind your ears or splash them into a running bath. Aromatics are the key. To experience them at their peak (and to lessen the possible acidity impact), chill them to between 8 and 12°C. Many offer the ultimate in daytime deliverance because they have some of the lowest alcohol levels among whites, in particular German Rieslings and lighter Muscats. Watch out for Alsatian and some New World examples, though, because they differ in this respect and could, quite literally, trip you up. These wines have a two-fold role as a summery sipping aperitif or a spicy match for Oriental food. They range from quaffers to thinking-women's wines. Judge each individually.

Rosés

Light, Candy-store Style

Made by taking the gently pressed juice of red grapes and fermenting it away from the colour-giving skins in order that the finished wine be the palest of pinks, these are cutesy, slightly sickly, simple wines that are best enjoyed so cold you can hardly taste them. Less good examples are made very simply by blending red and white wine together.

Smell/taste: confectionery, cherries, raspberry juice, strawberry juice
Colour: salmon pink or onion-skin orange
Look for: Rosé d'Anjou, Portuguese, Californian Zinfandel (Blush)

Fitting them into your lifestyle

Rosés are as much a part of a beach holiday as a bikini. In fact, this is often the only place many of them taste half-decent. Chilled is a necessity: 8–10°C. These wines are a friend to most foods and undemanding of those who drink them. They offer a similar satisfaction to sucking on a boiled sweet. Warm weather and outdoors are the obvious associations but there are really very few rules for rosés.

Dry, Spicy Style

Made from gently pressed red grapes, these wines may have more flavour than lighter rosés.

Smell/taste: red fruits, herbs and spices
Colour: intense pink
Look for: Provence, Syrah rosé, Cabernet Sauvignon, Spanish rosés

Fitting them into your lifestyle

A bit more colour and a bit more flavour complexity make these rosés more memorable. Drink them a degree or two warmer, and try them with hot food as well as cold. On the whole, though, they are as easy come and easy go as their light, candy-store-style alter egos.

Reds

Light and Fruity

This style of wine is made with grape varieties that do well in cooler climates and have thinnish skins. The resulting wines are typically low in tannin and colour. They are simply made, usually with little if any oak, and in some instances by a method of fermentation (known as carbonic maceration) that takes place inside whole uncrushed grape berries. This ensures minimum colour and tannin and maximum perfumed fruitiness. They are for drinking fresh and young, sometimes even chilled.

Smell/taste: cherries, red fruits, toffee, herbs
Colour: pale cherry red
Look for: Gamay from Beaujolais and elsewhere, Loire reds from France, Valpolicella and Barbera from Italy, Tarrango from Australia

Fitting them into your lifestyle

You might have been surprised to read that many light, low-tannin reds are best served slightly cold. (Cold tannic wines, on the other hand, would be an unforgiving oral assault course.) Beaujolais is one of the finest examples. Serve between 10 and 13°C. These are the outdoorsy, picnic-in-the-park options of the red wine world. Close your eyes and you could be fooled into believing you're drinking white. These wines can handle food and, of course, can come indoors, but they won't offer much warmth and comfort (alcohol levels are quite low at 12–12.5 per cent) on a dark, wintry night. They are early evening entertainment, appetite-whetters or lunchtime tipples.

Medium and Mellow

These wines are made from grape varieties that have thickish skins and offer a bit more by way of richness of flavour, complexity and ageability. They will have the necessary richness to handle oak experiences and will develop other layers of flavour from that.

Smell/taste: plums, toffee, strawberries, raspberries, spice, vanilla, farmyards, vegetables
Colour: ruby red; may develop browny fringes over time especially if, such as in the case of Rioja, the wine has spent many years in woody lodgings (oak barrels)
Look for: New World Merlot, Pinot Noir from Burgundy and the New World, Chianti and other Sangiovese, Rioja, Nero d'Avola

Fitting them into your lifestyle

Not difficult with the easy-going, cheaper versions of these chaps, which can charm the pants off us in most wine-imbibing situations and locations. Happy enough in your regular room temperature (14–17°C) – unless of course you live in an igloo – they don't mind being opened at a moment's notice, at any time of day. Posh Pinot Noir (particularly Burgundy) is a little more demanding, often requiring a tad more warmth (we are talking 1° more) and some pre-planned decanting to get it to open up, especially if it's been imprisoned in the bottle for a good few years. These wines are for food, for dinner parties, and, particularly Pinot, for white meat roasts. The more mature versions can compete in aroma and flavour with their food partners, offering similar meaty and vegetal charm. The best of these are wines to think about and impress with, not least in regard to the bruise they have left on your bank balance.

Dense and Dark

Made mostly with thick-skinned grape varieties that offer a concentration of colour and tannin – necessary for the long life-journey many of these wines make – these are heavy offerings that need food and can stain the teeth.

Smell/taste: many layers of flavour, which can include tobacco, pencil shavings, mint, blackcurrant, chocolate, moss, green pepper, stewed fruit, plums, leaves, cedarwood, truffles
Colour: almost opaque in their purply richness
Look for: Cabernet Sauvignon, Cabernet Franc and Merlot from Bordeaux and the rest of the world, Barolo, Barbaresco or other Nebbiolo, Tannat from Uruguay, Cahors, Negroamaro

Fitting them into your lifestyle

Some red wines, like difficult men, can be demanding. They require thinking about and looking after. If you handle them right, though, they can reward you well, because the best in this style line-up are some of the greatest wines in the world. These wines need warming up to room temperature or a degree or two above. They also need decanting in advance. Let them breathe and they will blossom. Let them sit around open for ages and they will wither and fade. The finest are wines for serious suppers or celebrations, for warming your blood on a winter-worn night. Savour with a meal (they love lamb or game) or go on sipping slowly afterwards (they like harder cheeses). They are thinking wines that magically shift, change and transform through layers of complexity in front of your very nose.

Peppery and Spicy

These are wines made with grape varieties that are characteristically cheekily spicy, which, when combined with the seasoning of oak contact, can have a piquant result. Sometimes rustic and earthy, often complex and savoury.

Smell/taste: black or white pepper, black berries and other hedgerow fruits, rhubarb, plums, bitter cherries, liquorice, leather, smoke, toffee; always spice
Colour: very deep red, sometimes with brownish fringes
Look for: Syrah (Rhône), Shiraz from the New World, Grenache, Malbec from Argentina, Portuguese, Southern French, Pinotage, Zinfandel, Primitivo, Amarone della Valpolicella

Fitting them into your lifestyle

These big bruisers can muscle in almost any time and make their presence felt. They want room temperature and they want it now; they want food too, lots of it, and they want it rich and flavoursome. These wines like it when there are people and smells around at barbecues, but they also don't mind nestling in on a cosy night with you and a heart-warming stew or casserole. They are nocturnal creatures (better drunk at night) and, unlike SAD sufferers, show off their best assets in wintertime. You have been warned.

The Rest of the Gang

Tangy Fortified

These wines have a wonderful citrussy lift combined with a yeasty depth (from the yeast *flor* that develops on top of the wine as it is maturing in old barrels) and a salty savouriness. They have some of the most complex flavours in any wine yet are refreshing at the same time, and are guaranteed to get your gastric juices looking lively.

Smell/taste: lemon, salt, Marmite, bread, nuts
Colour: watery pale
Look for: Fino and Manzanilla sherries

Fitting them into your lifestyle

Poor misunderstood sherry has long been pigeonholed as something brown and sickly, set aside for the over-sixties. Not so, and especially not so for these guys, who are light and lively and need to be served well chilled (9–11°C). I would happily drink them all day but their appetite-whetting appeal means these mouth-watering miracles are really role-fixed as aperitifs. Their savouriness matches them with nibbles, and of course the Spanish invented them for tapas. Any time of year, anywhere you like, these could kick off any event you can think of; Champagne's chief competition, in my view, but much drier and without the 'pop', of course. Don't get carried away, though, and forget the 15 per cent alcohol.

Sweet Fortified

Very ripe grapes that spend a long time growing up in oak produce these rich, sticky wines. In the case of Madeira, the wine is also cooked. These wines age so well they can easily outlast elderly friends and family members. They are, some of them, simply immortal.

Smell/taste: Christmas cake, molasses, smoke, toffee, dark red fruits and/or dried fruits, walnuts
Colour: deep devilish red or dark brooding brown
Look for: Madeira, Liqueur Muscat, VDN (*Vin Doux Naturel*), Oloroso and Pedro Ximenez sherry, Vintage and Tawny port

Fitting them into your lifestyle

Like grumpy old men or vintage cars, these wines need a certain amount of consideration and respect (and are best not wheeled out too often). Temperature-wise, though, they are happy at anything between 11 and 15°C. Vintage ports need greater TLC: namely, decanting them off their harmless, soily-looking sediment. These are after-dinner indulgences, either to be served towards the end of a meal with cheese and pudding, or as the final closing curtain on a feast. Yes, they are Christmassy, in fashion and flavour, but you should not confine them only to then. Great, rich, gob-filling wines like these should be enjoyed when the fancy takes you and the budget allows.

Golden and Honeyed

Wines made from ripe grapes that have often been affected by a unique mould (noble rot or *Botrytis cinerea*) which shrivels them and concentrates the sugars, these are syrupy and sinful and yet have an uplifting acidity at the end that should leave you aching for more. Some will last for years, if you can keep your sticky mitts off them.

Smell/taste: oranges, apricots, honey, grapes
Colour: golden
Look for: Orange Muscat, Muscat de Beaumes-de-Venise, Tokaji, Sauternes, Vouvray Moelleux, Eiswein (Ice Wine), New World Botrytis/Noble Semillon

Fitting them into your lifestyle

Liquid gold deserves respect. These like to be served well chilled (8–12°C). This is another oral indulgence that I would happily allow myself any time of the day, but their optimum opportunity to shine comes towards the end of a meal with fruit or fruity puddings. They can go anywhere with you just as fruit does (picnics, outdoor lunch parties) or they can stay at home and seduce your dinner guests – this they also do especially well with extravagant, rich pâtés such as foie gras and dangerously creamy blue cheeses.

Sweetness and Light

Also made with ripe grapes but not usually those affected by 'noble rot', these have naturally high spring-in-your-step acidity and aromatic freshness.

Smell/taste: grapes, honey, apples, pears, spice, citrus fruits
Colour: pale yellow or light, bright gold
Look for: Moscato d'Asti, Moscatel de Valencia, Late Harvest (Spätlese) German Riesling

Fitting them into your lifestyle

These girly-girl wines like to be really well chilled (5–8°C) to perform at their best. This can help to reduce their sometimes sharp-tongued acidity. These fillies like showing off most in the summer, when they reveal their delicate beauty. They are for sunny-day sipping, working very well with fruit and more sinful sweet temptations. The lightest can even work as a mouth-watering aperitif. Many of these gentle wines have easy-on-the-cranium alcohol levels too, in particular German Late Harvest Rieslings (between 8 and 11 per cent), making them all-day appropriate.

Traditional Method Sparkling

These complex creatures are required to undergo a secondary fermentation inside their glass bottle. Additional yeast and sugar is added to the base wine in order that it re-ferments, releasing further alcohol and – you guessed it – that all-essential sparkle (of carbon dioxide). Trapped in the bottle this gas has only one way out: when the cork is popped (and a glass roof smashed or an eye blackened). The yeast can spend anything from six months to three years working its magic in the bottle before the wine is prepared for sale. These wines are capable of unbeatable complexity with a myriad of maturing flavours and the life-giving, mouth-watering freshness of acidity that comes from underripe grapes grown in coolish climates.

Smell/taste: honey, nuts, toast, butter, apple, bread, biscuits, pears, peaches, red fruits, lemons
Colour: from pale lemon to gold
Look for: Champagne, Cava, Crémant, New World Traditional Method sparkling wines

Fitting them into your lifestyle

Somehow, with sparkling wine, finding a time or place for it is never really a problem. In fact, finding a convincing reason not to crack open a bottle of bubbles (besides the obvious pull on the purse-strings) is a lot more challenging. Like the gentle sweeties above and for the same acidity-ruled reason, they ask for serious chilling (5–10°C). There really is no comparable way to mark a significant celebratory moment than by the breath-holding build-up and subsequent explosive escape of a Champagne/sparkling wine cork. Having said this, this appetite-exciter of a wine, with its sweet 'n' savoury flavour (especially in older, vintage examples) and its dribble-inducing acidity, has, in my mind, a place before any meal, anywhere, any time you choose.

How to get the best out of your wine

Wherever and whenever you are drinking, there are ways to maximize your enjoyment and get the best out of your chosen wine, just as you might look to get the best out of your chosen man. Much sniffing and a bit of close inspection can reveal a great deal...

Look

First, take a good long hard look at the wine. It sounds obvious, but you do want to check there's nothing suspect floating in it. It should also be clear, not cloudy.

From the colour alone you can tell a few elementary things. A red wine going brownish around the rim is probably an older wine because red changes to brown during oxidation. Generally speaking, white wine that is light in colour is younger; if rich and golden it is either older or sweeter, or both. Most sweet wine is darker in colour because it is made from dried grapes, and therefore contains less water. (Exceptions are some sweet German wines, and the light, floral Moscatos from Italy.)

Swirl

You recall the giddy excitement you felt that time the dashing wine taster next to you remarked 'great legs'. Sorry to ruin it for you, but he was most likely referring to the wine. This strange compliment for a wine describes the patterns it makes on the inside of the glass after being swirled. To see what I mean, put your wine glass down on the table and, holding it by the stem, move the base in small circular motions to swirl the liquid around inside. Now hold the glass up to the light. As the wine slides down the inside of the glass, streaks appear. The size of the streaks, as well as the speed at which they fall, indicate levels of glycerol (sweetness) and alcohol. The thicker and slower, the higher the content of both. As with a woman, though, a wine does not have to have great legs to be great.

Sniff

Much of the fun of a wine is in its smell, something we experience as we put the glass to our lips, whether or not we stop to think about it or try to define what it is. The amazing art of smelling allows us to identify many thousands of volatile compounds, called odorants. (That's 'smells' to you and me.) Sadly, we have only one-fifth of the smelling potential of a cat.

To get a good noseful, swirl the wine around the glass (again). This allows air into the wine, drawing out and enhancing its aromas. Then take a good hard sniff. Already you will have opened doors to smells you never noticed when you simply poured a glass and drank it.

> **Tip:** appetite stimulates our sense of smell so you will be most receptive when you are chewing at chair legs with hunger.
>
> **Bonus tip:** women have a heightened sense of smell when they are ovulating, according to Professor Tim Jacob of Cardiff University, who specializes in olfaction research (smelling). So if you're clever enough to know when that is (it always baffles me), you can maximize your sniff power then.

Taste

The rest of the fun is in the taste – not forgetting the effect, of course: the way wine, as alcohol, has the ability to convince us that we are highly skilled karaoke artists or much admired table-top performers. As with smell, we choose whether we wish to focus on taste and analyse it, or just enjoy it.

Disappointingly unlike our clever olfactory network, our tastebuds – stored in papillae on our tongues – enable us to identify only five basic tastes: sweet, salty, sour, bitter and umami. This fifth taste might be as unfamiliar to you as it was until recently to me – it is a Japanese term referring to a savoury flavour that comes from amino acids.

The good news is that we continue to smell as we taste a wine. Our olfactory chamber receives and deciphers further odours through a back-door entry system during the tasting process, referred to rather impressively as retronasal olfaction. Taste and smell therefore overlap. Have you ever tried tasting anything when you've got a bunged-up nose from a cold?

The secret to getting the most flavour out of the wine is to draw air through your pursed lips with the wine still in the front part of the mouth. This looks absurd (your lips adopting the form of a small mammal's bottom) and sounds ridiculous (like a sink emptying) but it certainly enhances the flavour of the wine. If you practise it often you may get expert enough not to choke when the red wine hits the back of your throat, causing you to hurl it across the room onto your new, cream suede sofa.

Swallow

Swallowing, now that's the easy part. You can, of course, voluntarily spit if you plan to taste a lot of different wines and want to stay reasonably in command of the English language, but only if there is a suitable vessel on standby ready to receive…

CHAPTER TWO

Waffle

LANGUAGE IS A FUNNY AND FASCINATING THING. SO MUCH OF what we think and feel is conveyed to others by words, words that we mostly take for granted in everyday use. It's only when you learn a new language that you realize how complicated it can be. Industries have their own language, or 'jargon', which they use to describe objects or activities unique to them. Take computers, cars or aeroplanes, for example: I took a megabite out of the reverse thrust and clutched onto my rear flat for dear life. After throttling my USB connection, I was lucky to come away with only a zip disk and a well-worn floppy … See what I mean?

The wine industry, you will not be surprised to hear, is no exception. With such a ludicrously oversized variety of wines produced around the world, the differences between them have had to be defined by the use of specific terms: wine-speak, or 'waffle'. Don't forget also that winemaking is a science, and science, as we all recall from those heady days of test-tubes and Bunsen burners, has a language of its own as well.

We get wine waffle from a mass of different sources: wine guides and wine books, both great and small, wine columns in newspapers and magazines, both short and tall, not to mention snappy sentences on tags and boards all over wine shops, and the backs of labels on bottles all over wine shelves. The question is: do we need to understand the waffle in order to enjoy the wine? The answer is no. Language is not indicative of our ability to taste or enjoy wine – nor is it indicative of our ability to get utterly plastered, at which point language, even at its most basic, cab-hailing level, often deserts us anyway. But if wine, its origins and its immense variety interests and excites you, then getting to grips with just some of the lingo may allow you at least to peer round the side of the door into…what exactly? The all-exclusive World Wine Club, the one inhabited by well-spoken men in pinstriped suits with fat wallets and vintage charts as screen savers on their laptops? Think again, girls. There is no private, male-only members' club. It's just wine drinking we're talking about, and it's fun and it doesn't matter where or when you do it, where you get your wine from and how little it cost you – you are still entitled to know what it is you are drinking and to understand more about it if you so choose. Our sense of smell might not be up there with the cat's, but it is almost certainly better than that of the average man, and our (closely related) sense of taste is pretty fine too, so why don't we make the most of it?

We can all taste, unless of course we have a blocked-up nose or are unfortunate enough to suffer from anosmia (a damaged sense of smell, which also affects our ability to taste). What we cannot always do, however, is find the words to describe the flavours that are filling our mouth.

The easiest approach is to break down the tasting experience into smell, taste and aftertaste, the detection of which is shared between our olfactory area (at the top of our snouts) and our tastebuds (all over our little furry pink tongues). The major components of the wine to look for are these:

* fruit/food aromas and flavours;
* sweetness (or lack of it);
* acidity (or lack of it);

* tannin (or absence of it, in the case of white wine), and
* alcohol (as if your scrapbook of wine hangovers would let you forget), but this is pretty much flavourless and odourless.

The more you think about the smell and flavour of wine as you taste it, the easier it becomes to recognize similarities or differences between wines and to apply words to these accordingly. Take three white wines, for example, two matured in oak, and one in stainless steel. Once you have tasted all three, you should be able to see the similarities between two of them and the difference in the other, and invest these in your complex smell and flavour memory bank, so that you could recognize the 'buttery', 'toasty' and 'vanilla' flavour of the oak (see below) when you come into contact with it again.

As far as wine writers' recommendations are concerned, if you try a few of someone's suggestions and like them, the chances are you've got similar tastes. After all, the writer is simply sharing his or her own experiences by pointing out wines that are worth hunting down as well as those you should swerve at high speed to avoid. If you don't like the wine that has been recommended, move on and read someone else!

Do us a flavour

Women respond more to flavour descriptions than technical information when choosing wine. Women have even said that they would like to see wine displayed by flavour rather than by region in wine shops. Men, on the other hand, are more likely to be interested in recognizing the grape variety or region, identifying the percentage of the wine's alcohol by volume to the nearest decimal point, and finding out, to the minute, how long wine has spent in oak barrels before being bottled.

The flavour descriptions we read on the labels of

bottles, however, are giving us a lot of information about how the wine is made, whether we realize it or not. Here's what the flavour words are attempting to describe.

Flavour Waffle

Oaky

Describes the way a wine tastes when it has spent time in contact with oak. This is done to add another dimension of flavour to a wine and to mellow it through gentle oxidation (if done over an extended period of time). It is most effectively and most expensively carried out through the use of wooden barrels, although the more commercially friendly short cuts of putting oak chips or wooden staves into the wine can also be used in some countries (usually to less convincing effect), particularly for cheap plonk. The intensity of oak flavouring in the wine can be defined by the age of the wood and how it has been prepared (toasted). Newer, high-toast barrels give more flavour to the wine than older, previously used, low-toast ones. Almost all reds are matured in oak to soften them, as are most non-aromatic white varieties. Oak's most commonly encountered bed partner is Chardonnay. (If you put oak with aromatic varieties like Sauvignon Blanc and Riesling it can often dull their unique floral, spicy, fruity freshness – my advice is, don't go there.)

Creamy

This flavour and texture description might seem most appropriate for white wines but it can apply to many reds too.

* When grape juice has finished fermenting into wine, the yeast that aided the process dies off. Winemakers sometimes choose to leave the dead yeast cells (lees), often

along with pips, pulp and skin mush, in contact with the wine for a few days/weeks/months in order to add a creamy richness and complexity, especially to what might otherwise be a rather watery wine. Take boring Muscadet from the Loire Valley in France, for example. A step up in price and quality is Muscadet-sur-Lie, which simply means 'Muscadet on its lees'. Try it, if you haven't already.

* Malolactic fermentation, when the sharp, appley malic acid naturally occurring in grapes is converted to soft, creamy, milky lactic acid by lactic bacteria, introduced by good fortune or by design, is another way of enhancing wine. It is most often used for grapes with naturally high acidity from cooler regions of the world, and almost always for red wine, though occasionally, and increasingly now, for white.

Buttery

This can be an indication of either oak usage or malolactic fermentation (see *creamy*, above). It complements other breakfast food references used to describe wine, such as toast (from oak) and milk (from lactic acid).

Biscuity

Not a million miles away from the *creamy lees* above but used more specifically in describing Champagne and other Traditional Method sparkling wines. This word refers to the flavour in the fizz that comes from the extended period of time (average 9 to 12 months but easily longer) the wine has spent trapped in a sealed bottle undergoing secondary fermentation with dead and dying yeast cells.

Juicy

Any wine can be described as *juicy*, but the word is more often used for light, fruity red wines. Effectively it means plenty of fruit flavour, sweetness and acidity, which makes the wine both refreshing and mouth-watering, in one. Just like sinking your teeth into the flesh of a ripe peach.

Crisp

Typically a term for light, white wine, *crisp* refers to the acidity that makes the wine taste slightly sharp and highly refreshing. Think of crunching on a bright, green apple.

Spicy

This term, used for both red and white wine, refers particularly to the grape variety, some varieties being naturally more spicy than others. Good examples among whites are aromatic grapes such as Riesling, Gewürztraminer and Pinot Gris, and among reds, Syrah (Shiraz) and Grenache. Rhône wines are made with these red varieties and you can also find good, rich examples from Australia. The States' favourite, Zinfandel, or Primitivo as it is known in Italy, is also a spicy little devil. Contact with oak often brings out a certain spicy something in some wines as well.

Dry

How can a liquid be dry? Generally this refers to wines that aren't sweet, including wines that may appear sweet at first, particularly if they have a very ripe fruitiness to them, but whose final flavour in the mouth is *dry*.

Yeasty

Another of the *creamy*, *biscuity* school of flavours, this also describes the effect of the lees (dead yeast cells) left over in the wine after fermentation. In the case of some still wines and many quality sparkling wines (i.e. Champagne), the lees are kept in contact with the wine for long periods of time: weeks or months, or even, in the case of fizz, years.

Aromatic

A word used to describe wines made from grape varieties with distinctive floral, exotic or herby smells – think of your last aromatherapy massage. Examples of these grapes and their unique aromas are Gewürztraminer (lychees and rose petals), Muscat (grapes – yes, it's one of the only varieties to produce a wine that smells of grapes), Viognier (apricots and spice), Pinot Gris (floral and spicy), Riesling (floral, lime, petrol!), Albariño (floral and spicy) and sometimes Sauvignon Blanc (grassy, herbaceous).

Honeyed

This term is used for richer, sweeter white wines that have started to develop, usually with age and usually in the bottle, a more complex flavour of honey. Some wines, such as Roussanne and Marsanne, are honeyed from the start, as are most dessert wines, which are made from sun-dried or mould-dried ('noble rot') grapes such as Sauternes (from France), Tokaji (from Hungary) and Trockenbeerenauslese (from Germany or Austria).

Earthy

Surprisingly, this is usually a positive term, used for red wines that have an extra dimension beyond the flavour of fruit. Certain varieties are more prone to earthy flavours than others, such as Cabernet Sauvignon and Syrah (Shiraz). In cheaper, duller wines *earthy* can be a derogatory term and mean they taste a bit dirty. In classier, pricier wines, it describes a complexity and depth of flavour not a million miles from *smoky*, *leathery*, *vegetal* characteristics (see below).

Floral

Can a wine smell of flowers? Sounds strange but it can. Some grape varieties, particularly those used in white wine, can smell and taste like fresh flowers or floral perfume. Some obvious examples are Gewürztraminer, Riesling, Muscat, Müller-Thurgau, Albariño and Viognier, where *floral* often combines with *aromatic*.

Gamey

Certain red wines develop *gamey* characteristics with age. Think of the smell and taste of roast pheasant or venison steeped in its juices smothered in a rich gravy ... Similar flavours can be found in mature red wines, particularly older Pinot Noirs and Syrahs (Shiraz).

Peppery

Closely linked to *spicy*, and more common in red wines, some grape varieties are particularly *peppery*. Syrah (Shiraz), for one, often smells of freshly ground black peppercorns. Zinfandel and some Portuguese reds can also sometimes seem to be sprinkled with this seasoning.

Petrolly

It is hard to imagine that a whiff of petrol on a glass of wine could be an attractive quality, yet somehow it is. (Come to think of it, I've met a few people who get a thrill out of filling up the car.) Another description is *kerosene* (paraffin oil). But don't just take my word for it. Find a mature German Riesling, 1995 vintage or before, and have a good sniff. Vivid images of paraffin lamps and garages will fill your head, along with other fruity and aromatic aromas.

Vanilla

This means oak has been at work in the fermentation and/or maturation of a wine. Nowadays the majority of oak barrels used in winemaking come from America or France. American oak is more pungently vanilla-y, as are newer barrels. Can be overdone.

Nutty

Not too far from *vanilla*, in that it can also be associated with oak exposure (such as the great white Chardonnays of Burgundy or long-oaked white Riojas), this characteristic is more common in whites, and can also emerge from ageing wine in the bottle. A mature Semillon from the Hunter Valley in New South Wales, Australia, for example, is rarely aged in oak, but shifts from a citrussy, zesty, grassy freshness when young, to a rich, *nutty* and honeyed flavour after a good few years spent resting in your cellar.

Minerally

Some people (especially the *terroir*-talking French) say you can taste in a wine the characteristics of the soil in which the grapes were grown. Some cynics question their sanity. What is true is that certain very mineral-rich soils do seem to produce wines with a certain *minerally* character. That is to say, you can detect, for example, a slightly austere, slaty stoniness in wines from chalky or flinty soils. Chablis is a good example, as is Pouilly-Fumé from the Loire (which takes the name *fumé* – smoky – from the gunflinty soils in which its Sauvignon Blanc grape is planted).

Vegetal

It depends on the variety, but some grapes do smell and taste slightly of vegetables or vegetation. *Vegetal* characteristics are more commonly associated with red wines, particularly Pinot Noir, Cabernet Sauvignon, Merlot and Cabernet Franc (especially older wines), although some rather broad-flavoured, not overly fruity whites can have a touch of it too. As with most things, it can be bad news if it's overpowering.

Smoky

Could be oak, could be the soils, could be the grape variety, red or white... there are a number of reasons for smokiness in wine. It can be a lovely, dark, smouldering character in rich, red wines like a Syrah or a Cabernet Sauvignon, or an austerity and elegance in a Sauvignon Blanc, such as a Sancerre or Pouilly-Fumé.

Leathery

Red wines with a bit of age on them can often start to smell like a horse's saddle or an old and well-handled wallet. The variety that goes this way most often is Syrah (Shiraz), and sometimes Pinot Noir too.

Green

The unripe smell and taste from grapes picked before they were ready or otherwise overproduced. Some red varieties have a greater tendency to pick up this characteristic, such as Merlot, Cabernet Sauvignon and Cabernet Franc, as well as various whites. These wines can have a sharp, acidic taste. *Green* is largely a derogatory term, and not to be confused with *herbaceous*.

Stalky

Self-explanatory really, and even worse than *green*, this is wine with a harsh, drying, tannic character from the juice's contact with too many grape stalks.

Herbaceous

Not to be confused with *green*, though it sometimes is. This is a wild, leafy, aromatic character common to the white variety Sauvignon Blanc and red varieties Cabernet Sauvignon, Merlot and Cabernet Franc.

Meaty

A bit like *gamey* in red wines, this can also mean a certain spiciness too. Pinot Noir, in particular from

Burgundy, can become especially *meaty* with age, and thus a *meaty* smell can be indicative of maturity in a wine. More often, however, this simply refers to a wine's richness and intensity. 'It's a real beefy number,' you might also sometimes hear.

'Are you sure about all this flavour nonsense?'

We have looked at the flavour components of wine and explained how they derive from the winemaking process or from the grapes themselves at the heart of it all, but isn't it a little odd to say that a wine tastes of a particular fruit, or even of something else? Actually, there is method in all this madness. Grapes alone contain around four hundred naturally occurring chemical components, and these components can be found in other fruits or foods too. When grape juice ferments, the resulting wine contains an average of six hundred different chemical components, many of which can also be found in other food substances. Strangely enough, as we've already seen, it's only Muscat of all grape varieties that produces a wine that smells and tastes of grapes.

Let's Get Physical

Then there are the physical descriptions used to describe wine, indicating characteristics other than flavour that you can identify when tasting.

Body

This refers to the amount of alcohol and dissolved solids in a wine, and therefore to its weight in the mouth. The range is from light through medium and on to full. A thin, dilute, weedy wine might be light in body, just as a rich, concentrated one would be full-bodied.

Bouquet

Poncy word for the smell of a wine (and a bunch of flowers). Specifically differentiated from *aroma*, it means smells produced in wine through winemaking as opposed to the natural smells produced by the grape. Nowadays, the term is virtually extinct.

Mouth Feel

The texture of the wine in the mouth and the sensation it offers you. Ask yourself, as you hold the wine on your tongue, whether it feels dense and syrupy or light and watery, or somewhere in-between.

Structure

The way a wine is constructed: this is the combo of fruit, sugar, acid and tannin that you can identify as you taste.

Tannin

The mouth-puckering, teeth-staining, drying chalkiness of wine that derives from the skins, pips and stalks of grapes – much more obvious in reds (because they are made using these parts of the fruit). The tannins are there to give colour to the wine and act as a preservative.

Light

A *light* red wine has probably spent less time in contact with colour and flavour-giving skins. Its lightness might also be down to the choice of grape variety (thin-skinned Gamay or Pinot Noir) or the cool climate in which the grapes were grown (such as northern parts of Europe where grapes struggle to ripen). *Light* wines among whites include Muscadets from the Loire in France, Vinho Verde from Portugal, northern Italian and most German wines. It isn't necessarily a negative term and many light wines are mightily refreshing.

Length

How long does the wine's flavour remain in the mouth after spitting or swallowing? Can you still taste it minutes later, or did it disappear in a flash? Good wines have an aftertaste, and great wines linger endlessly. Poor wines don't hang around and offer an encore – often a blessed relief.

Finish

Linked with *length*, this is the word for the end flavour of the wine and the aftertaste.

Cloying

A wine with too much sweetness and not enough acidity is *cloying*. Another word that means much the same is *sickly*, and it's hard work to drink much of a wine like that.

Complexity

The greatest wines have this in abundance. They are wines to think about as well as enjoy. With more than one dimension of flavour and a balance of all the structural criteria (fruit, acid, tannin – for reds, and length), they truly satisfy. The best thing about these wines is they also have the potential to age, and may become more complex in doing so.

Passing judgement

To give an opinion on a wine, the terms we use must be evaluative – for example, it's got too much tannin, and not enough length. We can also have an emotional response, finding a wine thrilling, breathtaking or insipid. We can even attempt to describe its personality and character: moody, charming, feminine, masculine. These adjectives work through association. The word *feminine*, for example – stereotypically – suggests other words such as light, sweet, perfumed and delicate, which describe more directly the physicality of the wine.

Men's physical descriptions of wine often draw heavily on the female form. Words such as voluptuous, feline, nubile, virgin, blushing and curvaceous can be found dotted around their tasting sheets, sometimes even in reference to the wine... There is a whole world of sexual innuendo out there, and we women can have fun with it too. Fancy a glass of a big mouth-filling wine with firm structure and great length, anyone?

More importantly, wine tasting is a personal voyage of discovery and nobody else has got your tastebuds or your exact preferences. If you like dry wine and take a mouthful of sweet, your first reaction is likely to be negative, however fine the wine. It also depends on the wines you are used to drinking. If you drink only big, alcoholic Australian Shiraz then any light red from a coolish part of France, such as a Beaujolais, might seem pale, watery and insipid to you. Different interpretations of flavour are inevitable too. My idea of *earthy* might be quite different to yours. (I might have eaten more mud pies as a child than you.) For all these reasons wine waffle comes in for a lot of criticism. Wine descriptions are indeed deeply individual and sometimes only make sense to the taster. But 'tasting' remains the single most common way of assessing a wine's sensory properties, and what else can we do it with but our mouths and our noses? And the world would be a much less interesting place if we were unable to share our sensory experiences, even by means necessarily subjective. We might see the colours around us differently, but we use the same words to describe them – and so it must be with wine. One of the great mysteries of life.

Finding Fault

As a natural product, wine can suffer at the cruel hands of fate from time to time. Here are some of the most common terms used to describe faults.

Corked

Not, as is commonly misperceived, wine with bits of floating cork in it, but musty, mouldy, evil-smelling wine that has been infected with a mould, TCA. This mould occasionally develops in the cork as a result of a reaction between the chlorine used to clean it and the moisture and fungi content of the natural product itself. Cork manufacturers find it hard to prevent this mould from sometimes taking hold. The latest figures suggest that over 1 per cent of corks are affected: that's at least 1 million cases out of our 100-million-case market in the UK. If you suspect a bottle of wine to have been affected you are perfectly within your rights to take it back to the shop and ask for a refund. Likewise, if you are poured a corked wine in a restaurant, you should send it back. It is only by people doing this that the full extent of the problem can be identified. This will increase pressure on the cork makers to find a solution, or they stand to lose out to competition from alternative closures, such as plastic corks and screw caps.

Oxidized

Too much oxygen is bad for any of us (it ages us too quickly), but we need constant exposure to the right amount of it to survive. Wine is the same. If it gets too much oxygen it starts to discolour (getting browner) and can develop a stale aroma and taste. Take this to its extreme and you've got vinegar. Red wine can withstand oxidation better than white because of its tannins.

Volatile

Wine is made up of a complex combination of organic acids. A wine in which the level of acetic acid (the most common volatile acid) is too high can have a pungent, perfumed aroma that overwhelms the other smells and flavours of the wine. Like a volatile man, this characteristic in a wine is difficult to deal with. Chuck it/him!

A thought to leave you with…

'You can talk about wine as if it were a bunch of flowers (fragrant, heavily perfumed); a packet of razor blades (steely); a navy (robust, powerful); a troupe of acrobats (elegant and well balanced); a successful industrialist (distinguished and rich); a virgin in a bordello (immature and giving promise of pleasure to come); Brighton beach (clean and pebbly); even a potato (earthy) or a Christmas pudding (plump, sweet and round).'

DEREK COOPER, in *The Fireside Book of Wine* edited by Alexis Bespaloff

…just don't get so carried away, you forget to drink the stuff!

CHAPTER THREE
Wine and Eating

EATING, THE ART OF CHEWING AND SWALLOWING, AN ORDINARY enough task, yet capable of providing so much pleasure to so many. The range of food available to us now is immense – a far cry from the plain roast pig and common or garden veggies that would have spread across the tables of a medieval feast. Now we choose in our supermarkets from six different types of potato, which we can prepare in at least six different ways (as given in the packet instructions), and if that's not enough we can add to our shopping trolley anything from the sun-embarrassed tomatoes of remote Tuscan villages to entire Chinese banquets in a box…and don't even get me started on crisp flavours and cereal mixtures. I remember a time when 'rocket' took people in space suits to the moon. To accompany this immensity is an equally alarming array of wine options: miles of aisles to walk in your local off-licence or a forest-worth of paperwork to plough through in a restaurant.

In short, we are spoilt for choice. Small wonder we so often go with what we know, or the 2-for-1 deal that week. Perhaps you couldn't care less about which wine to drink with which food anyway. You know what you like and you go for that. Quite right. It all comes down to personal taste in the end, and only you know yours.

However, there is a fundamental truth that needs to be considered, and that is that good flavour combinations of wine and food are based on sound scientific and chemical sense. Certain chemical components of food work better alongside particular components of certain wines. The etiquette of food and wine matching might seem like tosh, but it's mostly based on common sense and scientific fact.

The four elements of wine (and men)

Wine, much like your chosen man, is made up of four basic elements – tannin (looks and body), acid (sense of humour), sugar (kindness) and alcohol (interest in sport, testosterone) – all to greater or lesser degrees. Each wine (or man), with its own unique combination of these, mixes and reacts uniquely to the components of any given dish (you, the woman) – improving it, complementing it, or simply messing it around completely.

The acidity (that's laughing *with* you or making *you* laugh) in wine is good for the digestion and for breaking down food solids. A high-acid wine on an empty stomach (laughing *at* you), on the other hand, is an open invitation for stomach-ache. Wines with comparable flavour components to the food in question (Have you got anything in common with him?) can either complement each other perfectly or be too similar for excitement (Are you perfectly in tune or do you bore each other?), just as very different characteristics can highlight the best in both or create a terrible clash (Do you stimulate each other or disagree about everything?). Between extremes lies a happy medium, where the combination is fine and reliable but not thrilling or particularly memorable. (Only you can decide if the happy medium is a good thing in a man!)

Wine and food

If the nineteenth-century Frenchman Brillat-Savarin is to be believed, 'A meal without wine is like a day without sunshine.' For too long in this country we have had too little of both. (Lack of sunshine we can do nothing about, but wine is something else.) Winemaking, and indeed the drinking of wine, has historically not been part of British culture. It's mostly too wet and cold here for grapes to ripen properly. And let's face it, fish'n'chips, our genius culinary invention, is notoriously difficult to match with wines anyway, particularly with heavy-handed vinegar seasoning. So we don't have the thousands of years of experience southern European countries have in growing grapes and making wine to go with food.

Long ago the Greeks began by adding pine resin to their wine, and the Romans honey to theirs, to make what they considered a palatable match for their strong-tasting, salty diets. These days, Italy, Spain and France pride themselves on their regional variations: wonderful, locality-specific combinations of food and wine determined by climate, terrain and environment.

There's a lot more to Italy, for example, than Chianti and Valpolicella washing down pizza'n'pasta. Truffles, game, risotto, polenta, seafood, vast juicy fresh vegetables and cheeses are the food you can expect to find there, and all these delights deserve – and have – wines to match. In the north of Italy, Piemonte is the culinary capital, but every region is rich in diversity. Most wine is produced in the south and in Sicily, where the sun encourages heady alcoholic heights, and mass-produced bulk wine is often sent north to add oomph to blends. Not just an accompaniment, wine is of course a great ingredient too. Like all great partnerships, wine and food help each other. Wine is a perfect ingredient in risotto and polenta, and they, in turn, act as ideal alcohol absorbers.

The Spanish have sherry to whet their appetite and

get their gastric juices flowing. With its acidity and often savoury flavour, it is mouth-watering and hunger-hastening, and the perfect complex partner to their tapas – small dishes with strong and varied flavours. Sherry is made in a range of styles from bone-dry and salty to syrupy sweet. Then there's Rioja, both red and white – often with extraordinary oakiness to suit their rich meat stews or paellas. No wonder they need *siestas*, to prepare them for the nightly *fiestas* of eating and drinking – few of which start up much before midnight.

Then there are the French, of course, who have wine at every meal except breakfast, showing just enough restraint to avoid pouring it over their cereal. The confidence they have in their culinary pre-eminence they also have in their wine. They take a real interest in the quality, variety and compatibility of both. There is wine for their seafood (Muscadet or Chablis), wine for their foie gras (Sauternes) and wine for their rich creamy sauces (White Burgundy or Vin de Pays Chardonnay), to name but a few. And where would *coq au vin* or *boeuf bourguignonne* be without wine? The French have surely cornered the market in cooking with wine as well.

As we now see so much of these fabulous, flavour-filled food ideas pouring out of our restaurant kitchens or piled high on our supermarket shelves, and have so many of these great and gulpable wines on offer to us, too, why should we not follow some of their proven guidelines – for they are the masters (and mistresses) of the art, the real experts in the field, surely?

Don't forget, though, that much of the most popular food in the UK these days comes from countries that don't make much wine at all, or certainly not for export. (Consider your local curry house or Chinese takeaway for a moment.) At first seen to be a challenge for any decent flavour-matching service-provider, the spices of Asia are now welcomed alongside vinous offerings from wine-producing worlds both Old (Europe) and New

(Southern Hemisphere and the States). Pacific Rim (Con)Fusion and various other newly invented food cults have lapped onto our shores, and our wine ideas have expanded to accommodate them. As a nation, we are becoming more and more adventurous with wine and with food. And that cannot be bad, since the real secret is experimentation.

Match and Mismatch

Here are some examples of the minglings in my mouth that were so utterly out of this world I thought I had grown wings, flown up to heaven, sung with the angels and returned to find all the washing-up done. Oh yes, that good. (To be followed by a chastening reminder of some of the disastrous combos I have had the misfortune to expose my tastebuds to.)

Love at First Bite/Slurp

* Spicy, aromatic food with aromatic whites – spicy food doesn't long for big, burly wines but for ones with character and complexity from aromatic or spicy grape varieties.
* BBQ and smoky food with spicy red wines – a sizzling combination of smoke and spice. Look particularly for ripe, warm-climate red wines to go with sweet barbecue sauces.
* Red meats and meaty reds – the tannins in the red wine stand strong with red meat, and they harmonize together. Also look for older reds from Pinot Noir and Syrah, which develop their own meaty character with age.
* Tapas with Fino sherry – the variety of tapas and the versatility of sherry mean you're guaranteed more than a few enchanted encounters.
* Foie gras with Sauternes or Tokaji – the sinful richness of foie gras is beautifully balanced by the sweetness of these wines, while the fattiness is cut through by the wine's acidity.
* Goat's cheese with Sancerre or Pouilly Fumé – a sublime combination of freshness and mouth-watering tang. Makers in

France are so sure they often produce both.

* Puddings with dessert wines – these two were separated at birth. Just try to find a wine that's sweeter than your pudding (or at least as sweet) or the pudding can make the wine seem slightly sharp.
* Fruit cakes and puddings with Madeira – the rich toffee nuttiness of this sweet fortified wine is a cosy embrace around a mouthful of dried-fruit-packed pudding or cake.
* Vanilla ice cream with Pedro Ximenez sherry – the very sweetest treacly sherry works like a naughty toffeeish topping.
* Stilton and Tawny port – the sweet nuttiness of the port stands up proudly to the salty tang of the cheese. Remember, this pleasure is for life, not just for Christmas.
* Blue cheese and sweet wines – as above, the seductive sweetness counterbalances the ridiculous richness of the cheese.
* Chocolate with Muscat, Asti from Italy or port – grapey or orange-scented sweet wines whether rich, light or fizzy love the softness of milk chocolate. Dark, sweet red or fortified wines lust after the bitterness of dark chocolate.

Relationship Non-starters

Don't go there.

* All dry red wines and most puddings – the sweetness of the food makes the wine tough, dry and aggressive.
* All dry red wines and creamy cheeses – the creaminess clashes with and exaggerates the tannins.
* Dry, high acid whites with most puddings – the sweetness of the food heightens the acidity of the wine.
* Oaky whites/tannic reds with uncooked tomatoes – the acidity of the tomatoes clashes with the oak and the tannins.
* Most wines with vinegar – the vinegar makes the wine, unless it's high acid itself, taste vinegary and sharp.
* Creamy whites or tannic reds with mackerel and kippers – the fish flattens the flavour and exaggerates the tannin.
* Any wine whatsoever with runny eggs (boiled or poached) – as the egg coats the teeth, the tannin and/or acid in the wine becomes awkwardly apparent.

General Guidelines

Remember that there isn't only one wine for every dish in the world (plenty more fish in the sea!). Often a number of options will work. Here are some general guidelines to help you make a decision.

Be Stylish

Think of putting similar styles together. Try spicy, aromatic wines, such as Riesling, Sauvignon Blanc, Viognier, Gewürztraminer and Albariño, with spicy, aromatic foods such as Asian or Fusion. Or put meaty reds such as Shiraz (Rhône), Grenache, Pinotage, Barolo or southern French wines with meaty stews, casseroles, steaks and barbecues.

A Weighting Game

Try to match light, featherweight wines, such as Muscadet, Pinot Grigio, Soave, Sancerre and Riesling among whites or Beaujolais (or other Gamay), Valpolicella, Barbera or young Pinot Noir among reds, with lighter dishes. Match richer, heavyweight wines, such as Cabernet Sauvignon (Claret) or Shiraz (Rhône), with heavy foods. Merlot is good for middleweight food. Be aware of special contrasting exceptions, such as chocolate (strong flavours) with Asti (light, sweet and fizzy), or light tangy Fino sherry with strongly flavoured tapas.

The Acid Test

High acid wines work well with oily foods, especially fish such as sardines or whitebait. They cut through the richness, making the oily food more palate-manageable. Try dry whites such as Muscadet, Albariño from Spain, Sancerre or other European Sauvignon Blancs, Pinot Grigio or other northern Italian whites or Vinho Verde from Portugal.

Sweetness and Like

Do justice to your dessert or pudding by serving it with a sweet wine. Make sure the wine is at least as sweet as the dessert. Fresh fruit is harder to partner because it often has its own raw acidity; a light, citrussy, floral sweet wine such as a Moscato or Orange Muscat will offer the closest match. Dried fruits, on their own or in a cake or pudding, are perfect with the treacly rich, dried-fruit flavour of Madeira, Marsala or liqueur Muscat.

Age Concern

Wines change with age, either in the barrel or, more importantly for us, in the bottle. Older wines develop complexity and increased layers of flavour; the vinous equivalent to laughter lines and smile wrinkles. Plain roast meats come into their own in the company of a mature Burgundy or Bordeaux. But a bottle-aged Semillon, having turned from citrussy and grassy to a golden, nutty and honeyed treat, should be kept away from the plain fresh fish and would be better served with a buttery, rich chicken dish. It is always worth checking the vintage on the label or keeping an eye on what's piling up in your broom cupboard or cellar.

Overoaking It

The strong vanilla-y flavour of new oak, especially American, in many modern New World Chardonnays can overpower delicate dishes – make sure the food can fight back. Oaky Chardonnays are especially good with rich and buttery-sauced white meat or fish, or barbecued smoky versions of the same.

Hot or Not?

The temperature of food alters the flavour – try the same soup cold and then hot. Cold, raw or lightly cooked food needs a more delicate wine choice than hot, fried, grilled or roasted food.

Saucy

The way we prepare our food can be more important than the main ingredient. Be wary of the wine label that says 'Best with chicken or fish' or 'Great with red meats and cheeses'. Matching the sauce to the wine is a safer way to play it. Chicken or fish with a rich tomato topping, Mediterranean style, would go best with a soft red or a rosé from southern Italy, southern France or Spain, whose ripe flavours and not too many tough tannins will balance the tomatoes' acidity. Roast white meats, such as chicken and turkey, are usually served in a rich, savoury gravy for which a good mature red Burgundy is more appropriate than almost any white (especially if the gravy has got red wine in it). Be prepared to put aside the 'white meat and fish with white wine and red meat with red wine' hymn sheet.

For All Seasons?

Allow the time of year and the weather to influence your choice. Even if you were to serve hot food on a blistering summer's day, you would probably prefer to sip something cool and refreshing. If you think a red is a must for your hot dish, then choose a low-tannin one, such as Beaujolais (or any other made from the Gamay grape), which would be happy to spend a couple of hours in the fridge cooling off. Versatile chilled rosé can step in here as well to offer enough juicy, red fruit flavour to compete with the food while lowering your body temperature a few degrees. Likewise, in the depths of winter, you are unlikely to want to freeze your fingers off clasping on to a chilly glass of something white, however appropriate to the dish it might seem. Look for a light but warmer red alternative in this case.

Cooking up a Storm

If you are cooking with wine, it makes sense to put a similar style on the table to that used in the dish. (And if you are cooking with wine, by the way, it's your prerogative to have a few nips – you'll find the result in the kitchen is less stress but more chaos.) Put the better quality version of the wine on the table, of course.

Style file

Here's my rough guide to which style of wine goes best with which types of food, for you to follow, if the fancy takes you... Have another look at Chapter One if you need a reminder of the wine styles.

Whites

Zingy and Citrussy

Wines: Sancerre and other European Sauvignon Blanc, Pinot Grigio and other northern Italian whites, Muscadet, Vinho Verde
Foods: light dishes, raw or cooked tomatoes, white fish, raw fish and seafood, salads, stir-fries, curries, simple pasta dishes, cold summery food, aperitif nibbles

Neutral and Smooth

Wines: Gavi, Pinot Blanc, Chablis, Chenin Blanc
Foods: cold soups, salmon, white fish with light creamy sauces, seafood, white meats, omelettes or quiches, pasta with creamy sauces, risottos

Rich and Nutty

Wines: oaked Graves or Pessac-Leognan (Bordeaux), New World Semillon, Burgundy, Marsanne
Foods: Grilled or roasted white meats, smoked salmon, richer pasta dishes, grilled fish

Toasty and Buttery

Wines: oaked Semillon, white Rioja, oaked Chardonnay from anywhere but Burgundy, Roussanne

Foods: rich buttery dishes, barbecued white meats, grilled tuna, roasted game

Spicy and Aromatic

Wines: Riesling, Rhône whites (Viognier), Albariño, Torrontes, Muscat (Moscatel), Alsace and New World Pinot Gris, Gewürztraminer, New World Sauvignon Blanc
Foods: Eastern and Asian food, smoked fish, stir-fries using distinctive aromatic spices such as garlic, coriander, lemon grass or ginger

Rosés

Light, Candy-store Style

Wines: Rosé d'Anjou, Portuguese rosé, Californian rosé
Foods: picnic food, salads, cold meats

Dry, Spicy Style

Wines: Provence, Syrah rosé, Cabernet Sauvignon, Spanish rosé
Foods: barbecues, spicy food, Mediterranean dishes, char-grilled vegetables

Reds

Light and Fruity

Wines: Beaujolais, Gamay, Valpolicella, Loire, Barbera
Foods: antipasti, tomato dishes and sauces, white meats, omelettes, cold meat such as ham, pork or pâté, summery picnic food

Medium and Mellow

Wines: Merlot, Pinot Noir, Chianti, Rioja, Burgundy
Foods: *coq au vin*, rich pastas, mushroom risotto and other fungi foods, roasted Mediterranean vegetables, white meat roasts, lighter stews, hamburgers, paella, rabbit dishes

Dense and Dark

Wines: Cabernet Sauvignon, Bordeaux, Barolo, Malbec, Portuguese, New World Cabernet Franc

Foods: lamb, beef, duck, dishes with dried herbs such as rosemary and thyme; for truffles, mushrooms it must be Barolo

Peppery and Spicy

Wines: Syrah (Rhône), Shiraz, Grenache, Southern French, Pinotage Zinfandel, Amarone

Foods: beef, game, venison, rich stews and casseroles, sausages, steak *au poivre*, chilli con carne, barbecued red meats

The Rest of the Gang

Tangy Fortified

Wines: Fino and Manzanilla sherry

Foods: nibbles such as almonds and olives, tapas such as chorizo, peppers, tortilla and so on, fish soups, gazpacho, prosciutto, salami, smoked salmon and other smoked fish

Sweet Fortified

Wines: Madeira, Liqueur Muscat, VDN, Oloroso and Pedro Ximenez sherry, Vintage and Tawny port

Foods: nuts, fruit cakes, mince pies, toffee or dark chocolate puddings; port shouts out for Stilton and ice cream screams for Pedro Ximenez

Golden and Honeyed

Wines: Orange Muscat, Muscat de Beaumes-de-Venise, Tokaji, Sauternes, Eiswein (Ice Wine), New World Botrytis/ Noble Semillon

Foods: dried and fresh fruit puddings (especially fresh apple and pear), chocolate cake, crème brûlée and other creamy puddings; Roquefort and foie gras cry out for Sauternes

Sweetness and Light

Wines: Moscato d'Asti, Moscatel de Valencia, Late Harvest German Riesling

Foods: citrus puddings, milk chocolates

Traditional Sparkling

Wines: Champagne, Cava, Crémant, New World Traditional Method sparkling wines

Foods: shellfish, fish and chips, nibbles such as crisps and nuts, blinis

Easy-going wines

A number of wines are particularly food-friendly and flexible, and get on well with all sorts of different flavours. Great for taking along to a dinner party when you don't know what's on the menu. Like socially adept friends, these wines mingle freely and easily.

Pinot Grigio/Pinot Gris

The light, Italian, pear-droppy version is called Pinot Grigio. More concentrated examples of Pinot Gris come from Alsace, the US, Australia and New Zealand. The variations in style mean the variety can cover many food demands, from antipasti starters to fish or chicken main courses. The richest Pinot Gris is aromatic, when of course spicy and Asian foods are its flavour match.

Muscadet

One of France's most neutral whites, Muscadet is like a breath of fresh sea air and thus holds hands with most seafood more than happily. Its easy-to-please nature means it won't stick out awkwardly among most food choices, although occasionally the acidity might be too much. Can be overawed by strong foods, though.

Riesling

Whether a delicate German style or a nose-teasing, pungent Antipodean alternative, this variety's aromatics-in-a-glass offering makes it Asian food's finest ally. It can be sweet or dry (and sometimes two in one), with generous spice and acidity, and in my opinion should go everywhere with you. Some New World examples may take over more delicate dishes.

Sauvignon Blanc

This fruity, aromatic, green-grassy fresh variety can make friends with salads and spicy food alike. It's one of few whites to make a great companion of creamy goat's cheeses. The more pungent versions from New Zealand and Australia need slightly closer attention when match-making.

Unoaked Chardonnay/Chablis

Despite often undergoing elaborate winemaking manipulation, Chardonnay without oak is actually a fairly neutral variety. This means it twists and turns as necessary to work with almost anything, particularly lighter dishes, white meats, fish and pork. Watch out as an increasing amount of Chablis is made using oak these days.

Pinot Blanc

Adaptable in the same way as unoaked Chardonnay, it can have lots of mouth-filling richness but not too many distinctive flavour distractions. A white meat or Chinese food option, but also great with vegetarian food, risotto and pasta.

Albariño

The Spaniard's best-kept secret is now available over here. A fresh, peachy, gently aromatic variety from Galicia in northern Spain, this is kind enough for delicate fresh fish but feisty enough for spicy food too.

Rosé

Often overlooked by all except holiday-makers, this is a versatile compromise between red and white, simple and fruity enough not to make too many demands on the eater. Best examples are from Provence, Spain, Eastern Europe, Chile, Argentina, Australia and California (especially for sweet-tooth slaves). It comes into its own in the summer with salads, lightly spiced foods, barbecues and light tomato dishes.

Light, Fruity Italian Reds: Barbera, Valpolicella, Dolcetto

These have their own sweet and savoury, wild-herb flavour, with softish tannins too, so work well almost anywhere, somewhat like 'seasoning'.

Pinot Noir

Mature Burgundy, having developed its own farmyard or vegetal characters, has had a lifelong love affair with roast meats. Young, fruity examples of Pinot Noir from elsewhere in the world, on the other hand, have easy-going tannins and can work well with anything from cold meats to hearty stews and even many fish dishes.

Merlot

The softest and plummiest of the richer reds. Tough enough to stand up to stronger flavours without over-doing it, it's an easy all-rounder with pizza, pasta, steak or game.

Tempranillo

A low-tannin red from Spain, found in Rioja and now appearing elsewhere around the world, particularly Argentina, this has general food-friendly fruitiness. It's good for most things but especially for vegetarian and pasta dishes, char-grilled vegetables, tomato sauces and even light stews.

Tricky Foods

Even easy-going wines can come up against a tough customer from the food family. Distinctive, unusually flavoured food with certain tricky chemical components can prove a struggle for even the most open-minded of wines. Either you try to beat them at their own game by matching them up with a wine that's equally distinctive, or if all else fails, dare I say it, opt for beer, a cup of tea or... a glass of water.

Artichokes

The very distinctive flavour of artichokes make most wine, especially red, taste metallic and bitter. If the artichokes are served with lemony vinaigrette, try to match the dressing with a high acid, citrussy light wine. Alternatively, try the takeover tactic with a very pungent New World Sauvignon Blanc.

Asparagus

The amino acids in asparagus are similar to those found in bad wine, so most wines are made to feel poorly in its company. Many Sauvignon Blancs, however, taste of asparagus anyway, so they and other fruity aromatic whites are the safest choice.

Broccoli, Cauliflower and Cabbage

These are high-sulphur vegetables – think of the stink that fills the kitchen when you cook them, especially if you overdo it. (Sulphur is used in winemaking, too, but in large quantities can ruin the wine.) These veggies are usually part of a bigger story on the plate, however, so you can be directed more by the meat and gravy. Cauliflower cheese is best with Chardonnay or Alsace Pinot Blanc. Cabbage, especially red, is good with juicy, low-tannin reds such as Barbera or Beaujolais.

Cucumber

With its delicate, watery flavour, cucumber is easily overwhelmed. It needs the lightest of whites, like a Muscadet or Soave. Remember it's usually found in a salad, a sauce or a soup, so always consider the other ingredients.

Spinach

The bitterness of spinach can make it un-wine-friendly. Find a bitter match in light, cherryish, Italian Valpolicella. For spinach cooked with egg, cheese or pasta, however, a creamy white might work.

Tomatoes

When uncooked, their abundant acidity rubs up uncomfortably against oaky whites. Try Pinot Grigio from Italy (after all, the Italians have a fairly loyal relationship with the tomato), or a Sauvignon Blanc. Richer, cooked tomato sauces are better with low-tannin, juicy, fruity reds.

Eggs

Typically associated with breakfast, you don't often have to worry about how eggs go with wine. Or they're used in cooking but not so you'd notice (cakes, pastry, dough, etc). However, should the situation arise, you'll find that runny-yolked eggs on their own can coat the teeth and clash with wine's tannin or acidity. The canny Burgundians found a solution by cooking eggs in wine (Oeufs en Meurette, see page 78). The wine acts like vinegar in poaching and sets the proteins in the eggs. I am no scientist, but it works for me. Serve with a more mature, soft-tannin red Burgundy or other Pinot Noir. Omelettes (depending on what's in them) work with light reds or unoaked Chardonnay.

Peanuts or Strong-flavoured Crisps

These really shouldn't share the same mouth space as wine. Champagne as an aperitif is altogether so delicious it's hard to care (Cava, Spain's cheaper version, can work in just the same way), or try a tangy, salty Manzanilla sherry. Fino sherry with salted almonds and olives before every meal is the safe Spanish solution.

Vinegar and Dressings

Vinegar with wine is an acid overload, which is why dressed salads and fish'n'chips cause wine-matching sleeplessness. Using wine instead of vinegar in dressings is a solution, and adding sugar to dressings or vinegary sauces can help. Balsamic vinegar, made with grape must, has similar properties to wine and is sometimes even aged in oak, but its intensity of flavour means it's often best off with a juicy Italian red. If your salad dressing is based on cream or blue cheese, you can go for a rich white, even an oaky one like a Chardonnay. As far as fish'n'chips is concerned, Champagne, Cava or other Traditional Method sparkling wines are great because they have naturally high acidity and yeastiness too, or choose a high acid, citrussy still white that can act like a squeeze of lemon and cut through the batter.

Cheese Please

Cheese is so often an important part of the ceremony of mealtimes and available in so many different flavours and guises from all around the world that it deserves its own special attention here. I've referred to some examples of wine-and-cheese wedded bliss already, such as Sancerre and goat's cheese or Tawny port and Stilton or blue cheese and sweet wine, but what about the rest of the *fromage* family?

Hard and Tangy Cheeses

Mature Cheddar and Parmesan like spicy reds such as Syrah (Shiraz), an oaky Cabernet Sauvignon or Vintage port. Parmesan is, of course, also a buddy to fellow Italians Barolo and Sangiovese (Chianti).

Waxy Cheeses

Gouda, Emmental, Gruyère and Manchego suit most reds, including Bordeaux, more rustic southern French styles and also Spanish Tempranillo.

Extra-smelly Cheeses

Epoisses: Burgundy reds, Pinot Noir; Munster: Gewürztraminer; all these and Pont L'Evêque: Tawny port.

Crumbly and Mild Cheeses

Wensleydale and Caerphilly go well with light, dry, unoaked whites from Italy or France, and, of course, with English and Welsh whites too (no, I am not joking).

Rich and Creamy Cheeses

Brie and Camembert like rich, fruity whites from Burgundy or Rhône, or lighter reds such as Pinot Noir or soft, plummy Merlot. Otherwise fizz can do it for fun.

Creamy and Bland Cheeses

Mozzarella and cream cheese – consider crisp, unoaked whites, rosé or light Italian reds.

Cooking with wine

With so many similarities in the make-up of wine and food, it stands to reason that wine should be an excellent ingredient in cooking. I, for one, add wine to almost every frightening culinary concoction that passes through my kitchen. I am no expert chef, I am sad to say, but I do like getting my hands dirty as far as food is concerned. I love entertaining and experimenting with ingredients, and most of the time, I figure, if you can't incorporate wine into the dish in some way at some point, then it isn't worth making.

There must be times when you don't get through the whole bottle. Perhaps you fall asleep in front of the telly after a couple of glasses and wake up with a stiff neck and a cushion imprint on your cheek, or you need a drop of fake courage before a date but don't want to turn up with boozy breath and a slurry speech impediment. You can, of course, cork it and bung it back in the fridge for a few days (even with red as long so you bring it out a few hours before you want to drink it), and the wine will keep perfectly well. But why do that when there are so many exciting ways you could use it in cooking instead?

First the facts

Wine and other grape-based alcohols add flavour, character and sometimes colour to food and can be used both cooked and uncooked. All styles can be used, from red and white to sparkling, sweet, fortified and spirits. Choosing a wine to cook with means following pretty much the same style principles as choosing a wine to serve with the dish. White wine with fish and white meat dishes and red wine with red meat are good basic guidelines but certainly not the law.

Wine is almost always cooked in a dish, whereas higher-proof alcohols such as brandy, and fortified wines such as port and sherry, Marsala and Madeira, are more often used at the end of the cooking process. Wine that is *not* cooked out tends not only to taste raw but wishy-washy too, rather than clean and condensed. There are exceptions, such as Champagne poured over fresh fruit or sorbets.

Red wine needs to be reduced (cooked down) at least by half. White wine, often lacking the complexity of flavour of red, needs reducing by even more. With any wine, the alcohol evaporates and the flavour concentrates during cooking, so that the finished result is both rich and mellow. Equally, tannins are concentrated by this process, so among reds it is better to use fruity, fresh wines rather than very full-bodied, complex or very tannic ones. Oakiness can also come out in the final flavour of the dish and can be distracting. Food ingredients that are high in acid, salt, fat or spicy flavours can overcome acid astringency or tough tannic bitterness in the wine.

The evaporation of the alcohol might happen gradually in the long, slow cooking process of a beef stew or a *coq au vin* or in the gentle simmering of a sauce. At other times it is worked off more quickly, such as when wine is used to deglaze a pan or brandy is flambéed for a classic steak *au poivre* sauce. The bubbles in Champagne will not last in the cooking process, although a little of the sparkle survives in chilled, uncooked dishes such as sorbets.

Fortified wines, more intensely flavoured, have less need of concentration during cooking, which is why they are often incorporated at the end of the cooking process, such as a spoonful of sherry added to a soup just before serving. They are also ideal for adding a kick to creamy puddings such as tiramisu, zabaglione or trifle.

Keep leftover wine by freezing it in ice-cube trays, to defrost later and use for sauces in place of a stock cube. It freezes more quickly than spirits do because of its lower alcohol content. Wine also evaporates at a lower temperature than water, so in a sense it reduces more quickly than water, and you might need more of it to end up with the desired amount of liquid. Alcohol in wine also lowers the boiling point of cheese and helps prevent the cheese's proteins from going stringy, which is why it is so perfect in a cheese fondue or a cheese sauce.

Acidity in wine coagulates the proteins in cream, resulting in thickened, creamy wine sauces. It breaks down the thickening potential of starches, however, so that a flour-based white sauce will be less thick with wine in it than just milk. Alcohol reduces the strength of starches, too, so you can use wine to lighten batter, to make pasta or dough more easily workable or to dilute a starchy sauce. Alcohol also gets to work on fat quicker than water or stock does, which is why it works so well as a deglazer on an oily pan when you are making gravy or sauces.

And now the fiction

You don't have to cook with top class, top price wine to make a decent dish. On the other hand, the quality of the wine you choose will be reflected in the final dish. Don't ruin a dish with faulty wine. If it wasn't good enough to drink, it won't be good enough to cook with. Corked wine won't taste any better in a dish, nor will anything that's been open so long there is a layer of dust covering it – by then, it will be fully oxidized, vinegary and horrible. The idea is to cook with something you would drink but not the best you've got in the house. Save that for drinking alongside your culinary handiwork (preferably a similar style to that you used in the cooking).

Cooking with wine won't turn you into a park bench wino, or even make you tipsy, because the alcohol has evaporated. However, it might not have evaporated completely, and the tiniest traces of alcohol might be left behind after cooking, so be cautious if someone you are cooking for is teetotal.

Not all foods work well with wine in cooking. Root vegetables, for example, can be toughened by it and will cook even more slowly than in normal boiling water. In this case, add wine towards the end when they are already nearly done.

The acidity in wine may tenderize meat but it also toughens its surface. Add it at the end of cooking, or remove the meat and reduce the wine separately, then serve them together at the end. Minced meat is more accommodating. I always add a good glug of red to a bolognese sauce or lasagne's meat filling.

Poaching

This is the process of cooking an ingredient in a liquid that is not quite boiling. The ideal temperature is just below simmering point at 85°C. Poaching is normally used for meat, fish and fruit. The poaching liquid can be used to make a sauce, or, if it's sweet, a syrup.

Bruschetta of Poached Figs, Gorgonzola and Port Syrup

Put six whole fresh figs (use dried figs if you prefer but remember they will be sweeter) in a heavy-based saucepan and pour in enough port to cover. Add a generous dollop of honey. Simmer gently for 6 to 8 minutes, basting occasionally. Take off the heat and allow to cool. Remove the figs from the liquid and cut them in half. Reduce the liquid by two-thirds until syrupy; meanwhile, toast four slices of ciabatta or sourdough bread. Serve the poached fruit (three halves of fig per person) on the hot bread. Cut four generous slices of ripe Gorgonzola, place over the figs and drizzle the port syrup over the top.

Oeufs en Meurette

This is a classic Burgundian egg dish. Putting eggs with red wine is anarchic but delicious. Melt a knob of butter in a tablespoon of olive oil, and fry a chopped onion and some pieces of pancetta (or smoked bacon) until the onions soften and the bacon begins to crisp. Now stir in a tablespoon of flour and half a bottle of red wine (preferably an inexpensive Burgundy or another Pinot Noir). Cook for 15–20 minutes until the sauce has begun to thicken. Meanwhile, poach some free-range eggs in half water, half red wine. (The wine not only flavours the eggs but acts like vinegar in helping to set their proteins.) Allow one or two eggs per person, depending on how greedy you feel; remember this is rich. Serve the poached eggs in a bowl with plenty of the sauce spooned over and some crusty bread on the side.

Classic Poached Fish or Chicken

To poach fish or chicken, use two-thirds wine and one-third stock (fish stock for fish and chicken stock for poultry). Add a few peppercorns, a bay leaf and some parsley stalks for flavour. Poach for about 10 minutes (until the fish no longer transparent or the chicken is no longer pink). Remove the fish or chicken, strain the herbs and peppercorns from the poaching liquid, then return the liquid to the heat and reduce it by two-thirds. Whisk in a knob of butter to finish off the sauce.

Chicken, Sherry and Green Olive Stew

Brown some lightly floured chicken pieces (skin on) in two tablespoons of olive oil in a shallow heavy-based pan. When the chicken is browned on all sides, remove it from the pan and keep warm. Add two more tablespoons of olive oil and a large onion, thinly sliced, to the pan. Allow the onion to soften, then add a standard wine glass of Manzanilla sherry. Bring to boiling point, then add the same quantity of chicken stock. Bring up to a gentle simmer, then return the chicken, skin-side up, to the pan. Season with salt and pepper and cook for 15–20 minutes. Just before serving add a generous handful of good quality green olives. Serve with basmati rice.

Poached Pears in Red Wine

Peel six nearly ripe pears but keep the stalks on. Stand them up in a large saucepan, pour in red wine to almost cover them and add a generous amount of sugar, a cinnamon stick and some cloves. Poach until the pears are soft, then remove from the liquid using a slotted spoon. Strain the liquid, return it to the heat and reduce it by half to make it more syrupy. Serve with the pears and home-made custard with Marsala (see page 85).

Marinating

Marinating is soaking food such as meat or fish in a flavoured liquid, such as wine (most often red), for a good length of time, usually overnight – so forward planning is required. In most cases the acidity in the wine tenderizes the ingredients. This is a great idea for barbecues, when simple grilling is all that remains to do to the marinated foods. Dried fruits can be marinated in a fortified wine, such as brandy, to rehydrate and flavour them, such as for a Christmas cake.

Boeuf Bourguignonne Marinade

Pour a bottle of French Burgundy into a saucepan, add a few celery stalks, roughly chopped, a head of garlic (in one piece, unpeeled), two chopped carrots, some thyme and a few peppercorns. Bring to the boil and cook for 5 minutes, then set aside and allow to cool. When cool, strain out the flavour ingredients and pour the liquid over the meat. Cover and leave for a day or two in the fridge, or overnight at room temperature. The wine you use for your marinade will make up part of the sauce (mixed with flour, stock and cooked for 4 to 5 hours with the meat and vegetables), so use a good quality wine.

Classic Beef Sandwich

Place thin slices of rump steak in a shallow dish, add sliced onion, garlic, chillies and oregano and pour over red wine and olive oil to cover. Leave to marinate overnight. Just before cooking, strain off the marinade but reserve the onions. Barbecue or char-grill the beef and allow it to rest. Cook the onions and marinade in a pan until the onions are soft and the sauce begins to thicken. Toast or grill some crusty rolls, pour over the onions and reduced liquor, and sandwich together with the steak.

Teriyaki-style Chicken or Salmon

Marinate chicken breasts or salmon steaks in a mixture of one part sherry, one part soy sauce and one part honey, for half an hour. Then cook over a very high heat, basting occasionally, for a delicious teriyaki-style flavour.

Dried Fruits

Roughly chop your favourite dried fruits and soak in Marsala overnight or until the wine has been absorbed. Place in a small saucepan, cover with water and add a little sugar. Bring to the boil and simmer for 10–15 minutes. Allow to cool and serve with crème fraiche or Greek yoghurt. Delicious for a boozy breakfast.

Marsala is Sicily's most famous wine. It's a deep-coloured, treacly sweet fortified wine made similarly to sherry and matured in oak barrels for many years. Because it is not usually hugely expensive, it is great for cooking with, enriching and adding sweetness to many dishes. An alternative for this recipe is Portuguese Madeira, which is in fact cooked wine, so has an additional smoky, burnt-sugar-flavour dimension to it.

Macerating

A similar process to marinating but involves the addition of sugar or sugar syrup. It's used for fruit. The fruit is not cooked but with the help of the sugar soaks up the wine or spirit and releases its own juices.

Fruit Salads

Most fruit salads can be spiced up with a splash of wine, especially sweeter whites. You can add herbs and spices too, such as mint for summery, tropical fruit, and cinnamon or vanilla for plums, rhubarb or other wintry fruit. Red wine is used less often but can work if sugar and orange juice are included. Think of Sangria.

Prunes

Cover Agen prunes (a wonderful variety of prune from France) with brandy and sprinkle with sugar. When the brandy is thoroughly absorbed, chop up the prunes and add to a chocolate brownie mix.

Preserving

Preserving with wine is a form of pickling, something normally associated with vinegar (which of course is produced by fermentation in the same way as wine). The acidity in the wine works as a preservative (preventing enzymes from working by flooding the environment with ions, for the science buffs among you). In this way, wine can help meat, fish and game keep longer in hot weather. Combined with sugar, wine, fortified wine and grape spirits make excellent preserving syrups, ideal for fruit. The higher the alcohol content of the wine the better it is for preservation.

Kumquats

Prick kumquats all over with a pin, place in a sterilized, screw-top jar and pour brandy over them. Leave to allow the flavour to develop for at least two weeks, and up to two months. Serve over warm sponge pudding with ice cream. Alternatively, place in the bottom of a champagne glass with a little brown sugar and top up with fizz for a wonderful cocktail.

Flambéing

To flambé, spirit or fortified wine is heated gently in a ladle or a small pan until the alcohol starts to vaporize, then it is ignited, poured over food and allowed to burn. This process removes almost all the alcohol very quickly, leaving behind a distinctive, concentrated flavour. The alcohol must be hot before igniting, but not boiling, or you will burn off the spirit too soon. Flambéing is for show more than anything else, but why not show off in the kitchen occasionally? Resist at all costs the temptation to set light to the hair of an ungrateful guest or forgetful husband…

Cherries

Melt a little butter in a frying pan, flambé with cherry brandy, then add a few whole stoned cherries and whisk in a knob of cold butter. Serve with warm pancakes.

Deglazing

A simple process by which wine is added to a roasting dish or frying pan after meat or other foods have been cooked there in order to dissolve the residue. The leftovers stuck to the base and sides of the pan are rich in flavour and are delicious scraped off and incorporated into the wine. The deglazing of the pan produces a concentrated liquor that can serve as the basis for a sauce to go with the dish.

Chicken Liver Parfait

Fry chicken livers in a knob of butter for a few minutes (cook to preference but I prefer to leave them a little pink inside) then remove them and deglaze the pan with a slug of Fino sherry. Pour the pan juices into a blender along with the livers, some capers, anchovies, flat-leaf parsley and olive oil. Refrigerate for a few hours before serving.

Madeira Gravy

Add a good slug of Madeira to a pan in which you have cooked a roast. Scrape all the delicious debris from the pan, add a little water and salt and pepper, bring to the boil then allow to reduce slightly. Add flour for a thicker sauce, if you like, *before* the water goes in. Make sure the heat is up high enough to absorb the flour and avoid lumps. Then add the water and seasoning at the end.

Sauces

Wine is often used for sauces. It can form part of a marinade and then a sauce as in *boeuf bourguignonne* or be part of quick reduction with stock in a classic sauce for fish or steak *au poivre*. Both processes allow the alcohol to burn off to mellow the flavour. With sweet sauces the rules vary more. A sabayon hardly cooks the wine at all, whereas a sauce made by flambéing brandy for crêpes will almost certainly cook out the alcohol.

Lime and Butter Sauce

Pour a glass of white wine into a saucepan and reduce by two-thirds. Add a glass of fish stock (or chicken stock) and reduce by two-thirds again. Add the zest and juice of a lime and bring back to a gentle simmer. Whisk in cold, diced butter, a little at a time, until you have a thick smooth sauce. Just before serving add a tablespoon of chopped fresh chives. Delicious served with poached or grilled fish (or chicken).

Brandy and Pepper Cream Sauce

Deglaze the pan in which you have cooked steak or lamb with a good splash of brandy and a tablespoon of mixed crushed peppercorns. Allow to reduce slightly, then add a good glug of double cream, season generously with salt and serve with the meat.

Port, Ginger, Honey and Cranberry Sauce

Put 150ml port into a saucepan with two tablespoons of cranberry jelly, a dessertspoon of freshly grated ginger and a tablespoon of runny honey. Heat until the cranberry jelly has completely melted into the port. Then add a handful of fresh (or frozen) cranberries and cook until the sauce has thickened a little and the cranberries are just beginning to burst. An easy sauce that is great with game.

Muscat and Orange Sabayon

Place two egg yolks, the zest of an orange, a tablespoon of caster sugar and five tablespoons of Muscat dessert wine in a bowl set over some gently simmering water. Whisk well for 6–8 minutes until the sauce is frothy and mousse-like, and serve immediately. This is delicious with mixed fresh red berries. For an even lighter sabayon, replace the Muscat with Champagne; you will need to add another couple of tablespoons of sugar to counteract the acidity.

Home-made Custard with Sauternes or Marsala

Heat, but do not boil, a large glass of Sauternes from Bordeaux (or a botrytis Semillon from Australia) or the fortified wine Marsala from Sicily in one pan and 600ml double cream in another. In a bowl, whisk 50g caster sugar into six egg yolks. When light and fluffy, whisk in the Sauternes/Marsala and then the cream. Return the mix to the saucepan you used for the cream and cook over a low heat until the custard is thickened and coats the back of a spoon. This would also make a sensational ice cream.

Other Old Favourites

Moules Marinière

This is made by steaming the mussels with a wine-based liquid. Melt 25g butter in a large pan with a finely chopped shallot, a handful of roughly chopped parsley and a large glass of white wine. Simmer for 4–5 minutes. Add the cleaned mussels and stir for a few minutes until all of them have opened – discard any that don't open. Serve with a sprinkling more of chopped parsley and all the flavoursome liquor.

Coq au Vin

This is a slow-cooking casserole with wine. Cut a 1.2kg chicken into pieces (or ask your butcher to do it). Using a large casserole dish, fry the chicken in olive oil until browned all over. Remove the chicken from the casserole and set it aside. Preheat the oven to 160°C. Meanwhile, add twelve small peeled onions and 200g chopped unsmoked bacon to the casserole on the hob and fry for 10 minutes, then add a couple of garlic cloves, a tablespoon of flour, a bay leaf and a sprig of thyme. Blend in three-quarters of a bottle of red Burgundy and 150ml chicken stock. Bring to the boil and stir until thickened. Return the chicken along with 200g button mushrooms to the casserole, transfer to the oven and cook for one and a half to two hours. Serve with mashed new potatoes or rice.

Mushroom Risotto

This risotto uses wine to bind it together and add flavour complexity. Soak 30g dried porcini for several hours in advance, then drain them. (Use the soaking liquid in the risotto if you like but strain it first through coffee filter paper to get rid of grit.) Melt a large knob of butter in a good splash of olive oil in a large saucepan, and soften half a chopped onion in it. Add the porcini, then stir in

175g arborio rice, coating it in the oil and butter before adding 60ml white wine. Allow the wine to be absorbed. (Adding wine before the stock takes away its raw flavour.) Ladle by ladle, allowing each to be absorbed before adding the next, add 750ml hot vegetable or chicken stock (depending on vegetarian loyalties; the porcini soaking liquid can be part of this). This should take about 20 minutes. If you run out of stock you can always use plain (but hot) water. When the rice is soft, add a knob of butter, stir in two to three tablespoons of grated Parmesan and sprinkle with chopped coriander or parsley. Serve at once. You can, of course, replace the mushrooms with other vegetables, such as asparagus, peas or beans. In this case, add the ingredients towards the end of the 20-minute cooking process; they need less time to cook.

CHAPTER FOUR
Parties

I AM OFTEN MISREPRESENTED AS BEING OF THE OPINION THAT LIFE is one big party. It's true, however, that I don't find it hard to come up with an excuse for a get-together or a knees-up. In this chapter I'll be recommending how best to plan and stage the wine at events like these.

The handling of the wine depends very much on the type of party you are planning. If most of what you buy is likely to end up across your carpet or dripping down your hallway walls then you needn't worry too much about the time you devote to selecting and serving it. If, on the other hand, you are having a carefully thought out, desperate-to-impress dinner for your despotic boss or interfering in-laws, then it's worth taking as much care over the wine as the food.

Supermarket and off-licence wine shelves are bursting with variety. It helps to have some idea what you want and how much before you open the door to the shop floor. If you're planning to make a substantial purchase, it's often a good idea to go to your local outlet beforehand and ask for a wine list to take away. You can then return home, put your feet up with a cup of coffee or, more sensibly, a glass of wine and pore over, at your leisure, the many wonders of the wine world on offer today. You can then make your considered decision, place your order for it over the phone or the internet, and return, in the happy, unhectic pace of your own time, to collect it. Better still, many local stockists will deliver it to you at home, for free.

Quantity, storage space and money

If you are serving bubbly, an average allowance might be a third to half a bottle per head, more if the guests' heads are particularly hard. Allow for twice as much white wine as red, as white is the preferred party choice, especially in the summer: so, say, two-thirds of a bottle of white and a third of a bottle of red per head. You could push these red and white boundaries if you are not doing bubbly. Don't forget, of course, to take into consideration the time of year, the weather (if you can predict it) and the food. It's better to buy more wine than you need, either on drink-or-return or to crack open at a later date when you've come up with your next ingenious excuse. You can always take leftovers along to your guests' reply parties in the future, perhaps to jog their memory of the fabulously fun night they had in your company which they never wrote or rang to thank you for.

If you want to serve bubbly, but don't want to spend a fortune, go for Traditional Method sparkling wine (Cava from Spain, Crémant from elsewhere in France, or the same grape varieties as Champagne but from the New World) rather than Champagne; they are often more fruitily approachable too (with less cheek-sucking, indigestible acidity).

The amount of close wine inspection that goes on at the event depends on the scale of your social undertaking and the interests and concerns of your guests. There isn't much vinous analysis at most big parties I go to, unless it's to tease me about my peculiar profession. But you could offer up the opportunity for debate by introducing some unusual wine choices. Consider aromatic bubbly Italian Prosecco or pink rose-scented Brachetto instead of Champagne, or Portonic cocktails (see page 106) rather than G'n'Ts and V'n'Ts. In this case, it's also a good idea to have something more familiar close at hand for less adventurous guests.

Buying in bulk is the way to make savings. Majestic Wine Warehouses sell by the case only but offer fantastic deals on large quantities. Most supermarkets and high-street merchants also offer a free bottle or two over a certain amount or a decent discount on a case or more. Check in advance that they have the quantities you are after before you roll up with your giant wheelbarrow hoping to pile on the pick-of-the-day.

Or consider increasing the volume you offer by making wine punches and cocktails using cheaper, non-alcoholic mixers, or ask your friends to bring a bottle or two themselves. Specifying what you fancy can make it easier for them and of course helps you too.

Tip: if you are taking a bottle of white wine or bubbly to someone else's party, and you want your host to open it then and there so you can partake of its riches, then arriving with it perfectly chilled is a transparent trick with an obvious enough message. With red, the message is less easily put across, so you have to hope your host has recently practised her mind-reading skills.

So you've got all the wine home now, but where do you put it? A cellar is a great invention but also a great luxury of space. You don't have to have one to have a party. If you are shopping at the last minute then a wide hallway can take a narrow pile of carefully stacked storage for at least a few days, as can the corner of a reasonably sized living room. Keep the boxes clear of any warm radiators: direct heat does no wines any great favours after a while. If you've got a private plot of outside space, guaranteed free of thirsty intruders and at low-level risk of flooding, then putting the wine outside for a day or two is a sound option.

Style and temperature guide

These are the temperatures at which to serve each style of wine (see Chapter One if you need a reminder of styles) to the greatest advantage. Serving temperature affects wine in a number of ways. The cooler the wine the more the smell is subdued and the more the acidity and tannin (in the case of red) is emphasized. Conversely, the warmer the wine the better you can smell it but the less you can detect its acidity and tannins. If, heaven forfend, you dislike the smell and taste of a white wine, serve it as cold as possible. If you dislike the smell of a red, make Sangria or mulled wine out of it (see page 105), or chuck it down the sink. Aromatic whites can afford to be served very chilled as they have ample aroma and are more refreshing that way. Sparkling wines are also best chilled because lower temperatures slow the dispersion of the carbon dioxide bubbles. Chilling light and fruity reds can give them a bit more of a flavour framework and as the tannins are soft they will still be easy to drink.

When it comes to pouring wine for your drought-delirious guests, only fill their glasses half full. This allows them to swirl the wine freely around the glass if they choose to (to maximize the aroma-enhancing potential of contact with oxygen) without spilling it all over your new carpet. With fizz, however, where it is advisable not to do any bubble-destroying swirling, you can fill the glass almost to the top. Good excuse!

Whites

Zingy and Citrussy / Spicy and Aromatic

Serve at: 8–12°C. Refrigerate for: 2 hours

Neutral and Smooth

Serve at: 9–13°C. Refrigerate for: 1½ hours

Rich and Nutty

Serve at: 10–13°C. Refrigerate for: 1½ hours

Toasty and Buttery

Serve at: 13–15°C. Refrigerate for: 1 hour

Rosés

Light, Candy-store Style

Serve at: 8–10°C. Refrigerate for: 2 hours

Dry, Spicy Style

Serve at: 9–11°C. Refrigerate for: 1½ hours

Reds

Light and Fruity

Serve at: 10–13°C. Refrigerate for: 1½ hours

Medium and Mellow

Serve at: 14–17°C. Close enough to room temperature not to need refrigeration

Dense and Dark

Serve at: room temperature, or a degree or two above. If the wine is coming up from a cellar or in from outside during winter, put it near a fire or stove for 30 minutes

Peppery and Spicy

Serve at: room temperature. As above, put near a fire or stove for 30 minutes

The Rest

Tangy Fortified

Serve at: 9–11°C. Refrigerate for: 1½ hours

Sweet Fortified

Serve at: 11–15°C. Refrigerate for: 1½ hours

Golden and Honeyed

Serve at: 8–12°C. Refrigerate for: 2 hours

Sweetness and Light

Serve at: 5–8°C. Refrigerate for: 4 hours

Traditional Method Sparkling

Serve at: 5–10°C. Refrigerate for: 4 hours

Bulk and emergency chilling

Chilling en masse is easily done by filling your bath tub or a big bin with ice. Ice is available in pretty generous bag sizes from most off-licences and supermarkets. But be warned: at the end of the evening you will be playing that infamous, arm-numbing 'fish for the few remaining underwater bottles' party game.

If you are last-minute, small-quantity chilling, you need a deep bucket containing water as well as ice. Water helps to melt the ice, and as the ice melts it draws heat out of the bottle. A light, fruity red such as Beaujolais can benefit from 15 minutes on ice. Put whites in for a minimum of 25 minutes for a proper chilling, especially if they are aromatic or high in acidity; richer whites can have a little less time. Fizz should have at least 30 minutes.

Boxes, cans and big bottles

Just as parties – and guests – come in all shapes and sizes, so too do wines. Wine comes in bottles, boxes and cans, and any of these might do for your party… though often one sort or another is more appropriate.

Wine boxes are party-perfect. Whether the wine in them is great is another matter. Wine made for this quantity at this typically low price is done so on an over-stretched budget. The grapes used are rarely of the highest quality, sometimes underripe and probably squeezed for every drop of juice they've got. This is bulk production and it doesn't walk hand in hand with quality. What it can offer, though, is consistency – you know what you are buying will taste pretty much the same every time, there is no risk of the wine being tainted by mouldy cork closures, and you can cater for the thirsty throng without getting corkscrew cramp. White wine boxes stack up quite neatly in the fridge, but they do take up a considerable amount of space. If you are short of space, put them outside overnight or in the shade during the day and then in a cold bath, after you, with the bottles and cans, just before the gathering gets going.

Canned wine, similarly, might be handy but the quality is usually far from classy. I also think wine is too high in alcohol to drink from a can, when you consider that most of us are used to gulping from them. What the can is, just like the trusty wine box, is consistent, reliable and accessible. White wine cans need less time in the fridge than typical 75cl bottles. Bung them in for an hour or in the freezer for 30 minutes and they should be ready.

As for bottles, it's not the size that counts, of course, it's the contents, but should you be tempted to go for size, here's a guide to what each holds.

Magnum: 2 bottles (or 150cl)
Jeroboam: 4 bottles
Methuselah: 8 bottles

Salmanazar: 12 bottles
Balthazar: 16 bottles
Nebuchadnezzar: 20 bottles

Opening time

The trusty corkscrew, invented in the seventeenth century for opening beer and cider, now comes in a huge range of guises and sizes. The Waiter's Friend is so-called because it is easy to carry around in your pocket and pull out at any time. At your own party, however, your little black dress may well be pocket-free. If you are not too concerned about carrying your corkscrew around with you all night, my recommendation is the heavy in weight and price (starting at about £75) but unbelievably easy-to-use Leverpull corkscrew. Two simple lever movements and the cork is removed from the bottle and then removed from the screw (synthetic corks can be harder than natural corks to remove from the bottle and to get off the screw afterwards). As for the myriad other corkscrews around, I find the cuter they look the worse they work. If you are catering for a crowd, make life easier with a decent corkscrew. Top tip: good corkscrews have helix worms. The 'worm' is the spiral itself and a helix worm looks like a spiral wrapped round an invisible cylinder. Steer clear of worms that are fixed to a central shaft like a propeller: they make mincemeat of your corks.

Glasses for the masses

Many wine merchants hire out glasses. Some require a deposit that can be held against breakages, or they might charge you a small fee per busted chalice. Shop-hire glasses are usually a standard, easy-to-handle size. For standing around drinking, one size fits all. Only concern yourself with different glasses for different colours and styles of wine for a dinner party. You don't want your guests drinking out of big boats; it means they will drink your wine far too fast and probably make a mess somewhere inappropriate. Besides, moving around to find a refill offers guests a great escape route from a boring conversation and helps to stir the social mix.

Hire glasses will probably come out of a cardboard box with a light sprinkling of storage dust and possibly a slightly musty smell too. It's a good idea to give them a rinse. If you wash them in detergent don't use too much and be sure to rinse it off well. A strong smell of detergent can ruin the delicate aromas of your finest wine, and turn something ordinary into something undrinkable. It can also create a film on the inside walls of the glass that will rob your fizz of its fizziness.

Alternatively, consider plastic cups. I have no problem with these at parties. They are cheap and convenient and don't break, and thus you don't have to walk around in thick-soled footwear for weeks post-party, protecting yourself from hidden glass shards. They are, however, very easily knocked over or crushed by bumping bodies in overcrowded spaces. It can be a good idea to have both and distribute selectively according to the estimated coordination skills and care-taking of individual guests.

If you are serving mulled wine, ideally use mugs.

Glasses for smaller parties

For smaller-number parties, such as dinner parties, you'll want to pay more attention to glassware. Choose clear, plain glasses so that your guests can see what they're drinking. All good wine glasses should be tapered towards the top to allow you to swirl wildly with a reduced risk of covering your clothes, at the same time allowing the aromas to be channelled in a more direct route to the eagerly receiving nose. Glasses should have a stem that is long enough to hold easily so that you do not clasp your mitts round the bowl and warm the chilled contents. To really look the part, and I never find this very easy or comfortable, the 'correct' place to hold a glass is by the base. I tend to have trouble with wobbling when I try this, especially when the glass is top-heavy.

Fizz flutes are a luxury but one that pays its way in aesthetic appeal as well as bubble benefit. Their long tapered shape encourages a narrow, steady stream of fine beads.

White and red wines can be served in the same size glass, although the tradition is to have a bigger-bowled glass for red. This is because of its more complex chemical make-up and its release-seeking layers of aroma. This need for aeration is also why red wine is decanted more often than white, as well as, sometimes, to divorce it from harmless but undesirable sediment (a build-up of solid colour and tannin particles found in older wines).

Dessert wines and fortified wines are by their sweet and/or strong nature difficult to drink in large amounts, so they are usually served in smaller vessels. If I could have it my way, though, I'd always serve these wonders in giant aroma-releasing goblets.

To decant or not

Decanting is an ancient art and one, like Feng Shui, which many people don't understand. The truth is you can decant any wine into an easy pouring vessel such as a jug if you think it is easier to serve that way, or nicer, or you just want to hide the giveaway wine labels. There are two main reasons for decanting, however: to aerate the wine (getting oxygen in to interact with the liquid and draw out its often restrained aromas and flavours), and to separate the wine from any sediment (in the case of ports and old reds). Some wines therefore benefit more than others from being transferred to a broad-based serving vessel. Light white wines might be overwhelmed by too much air, so it's best not to bother. Also, they prefer to be served chilled and warm up quickly in a jug or decanter.

Decanting comes into its own for big tannic reds such as Bordeaux, Barolo, spicy Rhône or Australian Shiraz. Tip the decanter or jug on its side and pour the wine down the inside of the vessel so the liquid fans out and achieves maximum aeration. Do this about an hour before you serve it. Beware, though, that some old, lighter red wines, like old people, are frail and delicate. Too much oxygen will ruin them almost immediately, so it might be best not to put them through the rigours of decanting at all, or if you do then serve them almost immediately. Lighter, more vulnerable reds are Burgundy (or other Pinot Noirs), Chianti and Rioja.

If you are decanting because of sediment, you need first to arrange for the sediment to rest at the bottom of the bottle by leaving it upright for a day or two. Then pour the wine slowly from the bottle into the jug or decanter, leaving the gritty mush behind. To spot when the sediment gets near to the neck of the bottle, i.e. when to stop, you can light the neck with a torch from underneath. Or use a candle for atmosphere: very feather quills and Samuel Pepys. Sediment won't do you any harm, but it's not nice to chew on. By the way, wines that have been well filtered before bottling are less likely to produce sediment, but they are also less likely to become interesting and complex over time.

You may have been advised (by a number of old wives) that you can open a bottle in advance and leave it to aerate without decanting. The surface area of the neck of the bottle is so small that nothing much happens to the wine in this instance, so it's a pretty pointless exercise. If you want to get air into your wine then go for the full Monty decanting operation. Otherwise just open and pour.

The morning after

Remember how you vowed never to go there again? Yet we always seem to. Another party, another hangover, and each feels worse than the one before. We probably also behaved in a way we would rather not be reminded of (ever), though if this is the case for you, you might need to be reading a different book. Let's look at practicalities.

I am a big believer in recycling. Locate your nearest bins in advance of a big party and make sure you've saved plenty of cardboard boxes from your wine orders to put the empties in, or if your local council collects make sure you've got space to keep the bottles in and then remember to put them out on the right day. If you are taking them to the bins yourself, and nursing a cranium-crunching hangover, you might want to invest in a pair of ear defenders. You'll have to take off the dark glasses, though, however bright the light is for your bloodshot eyes, to make sure you correctly colour-coordinate bottle and bin.

Unopened leftovers are easy. Take them back to the shop if you managed to set up a deal for returns, or keep them on standby for next time (and we all know there will be one of those), or take one or two along to the next BAB (Bring A Bottle) party you go to or BYO (Bring Your Own) restaurant you visit.

Opened leftover bottles can present a serious health hazard and should always be checked for stray cigarette ends and peanuts. Any wines that you or your guests were sober or coordinated enough to recork at the time will be all set for Round Two. If you have any desire for wine ever again, then you can drink these up over the next few days. Alternatively, if you have an appetite for cooking, you can bung them in a dish for dinner (see Chapter Three). If there is no cork in the top, my advice is sink it. By this I mean pour it down the sink, not drink it. Wine left open overnight will start to oxidize. It will have lost its freshness and fruitiness, and even if it looks free of awkward-to-swallow intrusions, you can't guarantee what or who got near it when you weren't looking. Play it safe.

Champagne can be resealed with a champagne stopper or just a teaspoon, though how you could find yourself needing to reseal Champagne is a mystery. Believe it or not, and I still can't really, the teaspoon method does work, keeping the sparkle for at least three days.

As for cleaning all those gloriously unharmed glasses – now, there is an arduous task. Most glasses these days are dishwasher proof but the *best* way to clean them is by hand in very hot water (use gloves), without too much washing-up liquid, then rinse them in cold water and dry with a reserved-for-glasses tea towel. Pay particular care if you've gone all out and proffered your finest crystal to impress your guests. Rinse the crystal glasses gently in warm water, allow to drain, then upturn them and leave to dry off in the gentle caress of nature's breeze …

The occasions

Now, individual attention to specific party proposals and other social gatherings.

House Party

If this is wall-to-wall bodies, resulting in scenes of total devastation and carnage, then worrying about exact serving temperatures and made-to-measure drinking vessels is probably rather pointless. What you *do* need is to make sure there is enough to drink for the house-wrecking hordes and in enough variety too. It's often a generous idea to have a bit of bubbly to reward the first arrivals. For a big gathering, you don't have to buy Champagne (to a certain extent you are always paying over the odds for the name), but instead get more for your money of ripe-tasting New World sparkling wine (made in the same Traditional Method) or Cava from Spain or Crémant from (other parts of) France.

If you plan to lay on bitesize nibbles, creative canapés or just big bowls of crisps and peanuts, don't flap too much about pairing them up with your wines. Many of these moreish distractions, peanuts and olives in particular, crucify most wines anyway. If you've got a huge range of intricate eats, it's almost impossible to find wines that are going to match all the flavours, so go for an easy, refreshing, good all-rounder.

One such all-rounder – and please, read me out – is sherry. This much maligned and misunderstood fortified wine should not be reserved for the retired. Fresh, young, well-chilled Fino and Manzanilla are mouth-wateringly citrussy and delicious. With mixed nibbles, nuts, olives, canapés or anything remotely tapas-like, do yourself a big favour Spanish-style and indulge in one of the wine world's greatest inventions. The only thing to remember, before you forget everything including your name and address, is that the alcohol in these wines starts at 15 per cent.

White wine, not red, is the preferred party option, so make sure you've organized the chilling (warm, acidic white wine is capable only of quenching the thirst of the devil, whom I presume you have not invited). Choose whites of average alcohol levels (12–12.5 per cent) that are refreshing, dry and not too oaky. A good trick is to start with something a bit more special and costly, such as Sancerre, Pouilly Fumé, Sauvignon Blanc from the New World – New Zealand, Australia, Chile (£1 or so cheaper generally), USA or South Africa – or not too oaky Semillon. Then, when the party is in full swing and the guests are starting to sway, bring out the less impressive support team. Bag-in-box wines are easy, reliable, money-saving back-ups, and also useful up front if you find yourself catering for the 5,000 without the 'water into wine' miracle-performing support of the Lord. They'll save your cork-arm too. And if you are serving bottles, and you're confident of the reliability factor of those who said yes to your invitation or the just-turning-up probability of those who didn't reply, then avoid devoting your entire evening to a conversation with a corkscrew by opening and recorking a lot of the wines in advance. Then you can relax and party.

It's always good to have some red on hand for those who can't stomach white or for your more hardcore guests to trade up to/pass out with later on. Stock up on lighter, fruitier reds rather than big, tannic, headache-inducing blockbusters. Besides which, there is nothing worse than leaving a party (particularly if you are going on to another one) with blackened teeth and blood-stained-looking lips. See Chapter One for more ideas, but anything from Beaujolais (a white wine in red wine's clothing) to Chianti, Valpolicella or Kiwi Pinot Noir will suffice. A Bulgarian red might be just the thing for those with less discerning, 'hic, had quite a few already, thanks' palates.

Mass catering is also a perfect opportunity to try out and show off a range of wine-cocktail-making techniques (while increasing volume and keeping expense down). Here are a few ideas to jazz up dreary wines. Remember that presentation can be more impressive than costly ingredients. Think about how to make your cocktails look good, such as by decorating them with fruit.

Summer Punches

Unoaked, light white wine (spicy, aromatic varieties are especially good) diluted to taste with elderflower cordial and apple juice.

Light red (such as Beaujolais) with a few generous table-spoons of crushed cranberries, fresh mint leaves and lots of ice: super refreshing.

Pimm's Cup: a spirit measure of Pimm's topped with ginger ale, over ice, garnished with a squeeze of lemon and a slice of cucumber. Feel free to add strawberries, oranges and any other fruit life you fancy.

Summer: Champagne Cocktails

Stretch out your fizz drinking allowance by serving three-quarters of a flute topped with peach juice (Bellini, traditionally made with the Italian sparking wine Prosecco), orange juice (Buck's Fizz), or, one of my absolute favourites, Guinness (Black Velvet). It doesn't have to be Champagne for Buck's Fizz or Black Velvet, but it can be more fun if it is.

Winter: White Mulled Wine

Sounds unusual, but white wine can work just as well as red. You need to use a different set of herbs and spices. Pour a bottle of unoaked white wine (more depending on guest numbers) into a large, heavy-based saucepan, add three tablespoons of runny honey, a small bunch of fresh thyme and rosemary and three slices of unwaxed lemon. Heat until warm, do not allow to boil, and serve. To protect guests' hands from the heat, use polystyrene cups or get hold of handle attachments for plastic cups, or best of all use china mugs.

Winter: Red Mulled Wine

Mulled wine spices include cinnamon sticks, allspice and nutmeg, so be sure to include a little of each of these, plus two oranges pierced with cloves (the hedgehog look) and one unwaxed lemon, sliced. Use a bottle or two of a spicy red wine (a Shiraz from Australia or a Syrah from the Rhône), and spice it up further with a slug of brandy as well. Warm the mix in a heavy-based saucepan for at least half an hour before serving but don't allow it to boil and cover it with a lid to keep the alcohol from evaporating (and taking the fun with it). Serve in receptacles as above.

Big Birthday Bash

Happy Birthday! It's time to celebrate in style. If there's to be a great gang of you then the same laidback rules apply as with a house party. If it is an important birthday and you want to make it memorable (or at least the early part of the proceedings), be adventurous with your wine choices. Go for Champagne, if you are feeling flush, and make some fun Champagne cocktails (see above). A few unusual fizzies you could use to flirt with – unusual in that they are red – are the light but fruity strawberry and roses Brachetto from northern Italy, or the rich blackberry jam and spice sparkling Shiraz from Australia. These reds should be served chilled but a few degrees warmer than you would serve white or rosé bubbles. Guaranteed to get the guests talking.

Now is your time to steer traitors of the vine away from the monotony of V'n'Ts and or G'n'Ts towards exceptionally palatable Portonic (flavour-filled and refreshing, and better than most straight white port which is not worth drinking on its own). For this you need white port, tonic water, ice and a generous slice of lemon. Mix as you would a G or a V 'n'T.

With white wines, why not try some of the more unusual aromatic varieties of Riesling, Muscat, Gewürztraminer (all can be found from Alsace and now increasingly New World countries too), or the prettily perfumed Albariño from Rias Biaxas in northern Spain? There are also many exciting Italian varieties or blends of varieties: look for the romantic names of Verdicchio, Gavi, Greco di Tufo, Vernaccia, Malvasia or Arneis.

For reds, keep tannin levels low in your choices. Have fun with the red sparkling suggestions above, or go for light and fruity, or medium and mellow styles (see Chapter One).

Housewarming

Could be another opportunity for house-party chaos, especially if you've moved into a hollow shell and haven't started decorating yet. My suspicion is that if you moved into somewhere that's just been done up, the last thing you want is permanent reminders of your clumsiest or most wine-soaked guests. I'd make it as white-wine dominant a party as possible, and ensure there is plenty of clear space available to put down glasses. Low-tannin red wine has less depth of colour and will be less tricky to shift out of your beige carpet should a catastrophe happen. As with any catering en masse get organized by ordering from the suppliers well in advance. Glasses and ice can come from them too.

Barbecue

The great British barbie, weather permitting. With the feisty flavours of char-grilling and chilli sauce, you don't have to worry too much about the sophistication of your wines. Make sure you've got plenty of spicy, flavour-rich reds to keep up, as well as some well-chilled rosé (it gets on with almost everything) and a few light, aromatic whites or some Sauvignon Blanc to go with the salad side of things. Use ice buckets or bins full of ice (depending on quantities) and plastic cups. Bag-in-box or canned wine can have a place here too. Barbecues should be laidback affairs. Just keep an eye on how much wine your flame controller is getting stuck into.

Valentine's Day

It's more than likely – knowing men a little, as I do – that you will be the organizer of your cosy little soirée à deux. But if you are fortunate enough to have plucked yourself one of the few remaining chivalrous romantics around, then give him this list of suggestions and he can coordinate proceedings – unless, of course, you prefer surprises, in which case you'd better skip this bit. All is dependent on the menu, so these guidelines are vague, but should at least give you some ideas for the structure of the evening's imbibing. After a drop of passion-pink sparkling rosé (if you choose Cava then the rosé is called *rosado*), why not move on to a light but fruity, maybe slightly aromatic white (a Riesling from anywhere in the world, an Albariño from Spain, a Pinot Grigio/Gris from Italy/elsewhere) or, more classically, a Sancerre or Chablis from France. As you reach your main course, spice things up with a fruity, spicy red (unless you are having a creamy, white fish dish, in which case go for an oaky white), such a New World Shiraz – lots of alcohol to aid seduction, should you be needing a helping hand – or if you like lighter wines but still with the sweet scent of oak, pick a Rioja from Spain. Pudding time is where the fun really kicks in. Go wild on sticky dessert wines or fortifieds; port, sweet sherry, Madeira, Vin Doux Naturel from France, Antipodean Liqueur Muscat, Muscat Beaumes-de-Venise, Sauternes, Tokaji are just a few of the sweet seducers you can choose from. Serve with your dessert of choice, poured over ice cream or just each other… I'll leave it there, I think.

I needn't state the obvious (best glasses, linen, flowers, etc). How could he fail to adore you?

Engagement Party

Typically a stand-around drinks occasion. Of course, a celebration like this suggests fizz but it doesn't have to mean Champagne. Again, look to the New World for cheaper, often riper alternatives, or to Spain for Cava. Mix these with juices such as orange (Buck's Fizz) or peach (Bellini) or serve them on their own. Hire/borrow a bulk lot of champagne flutes. Have some easy-drinking whites chilled down as well, such as Pinot Grigio or unoaked Chardonnay. Remember, you don't need to go all out on the engagement party. It's just the warm-up session for the main event.

Hen Night

My involvement on these occasions has always been to ensure that the hen gets extraordinarily drunk. She'll need Champagne, which should go to her head fastest, especially if drunk through a straw from a mini bottle (20cl), as released by some of the more street-savvy Champagne houses: Pommery (Pop), Piper Heidsieck (Baby Piper).

If you are planning a girlie meal, then it depends what you are eating, of course, but as long as there is a constant supply of fizz, white and red wine and something sticky and sinful for afters, then she should be a happy hen (at least until morning).

If you are planning a weekender, pace yourselves. Plan ahead to stock up the fridge with a range of light whites, and the cellar or corner of the castle (or whatever it is you've taken over) with heavier reds for the stayers in the girl-power group. Also, make sure there are plenty of non-alcoholic alternatives and a direct and constant supply of good water.

Wedding Reception

The big day has arrived. As with all wedding plans, the wine order must be placed well in advance. Mention the occasion and you might even get a generous, congratulatory discount. Romantic rosé fizz or rosé wines (depending on budget) are the must-have aperitif. Depending how long you plan to stand around admiring hats, half a bottle a head is a suitable average. A classic white should follow – like a Sancerre or Chablis and then maybe a more modern, New World red, such as an Australian Shiraz or a Californian Cabernet. Finally something sweet and sticky to go with the pudding and wedding cake. Choose carefully if it's chocolate-based, as this can be a hard match. A Liqueur Muscat from Australia or Tokaji from Hungary would make the unforgettable day more unforgettable. It is unlikely that the more sensible bride, groom, parents/in-laws or speechmakers will want to drink too much on this special day, so factor that into your calculations of a bottle per person for the night (after the fizz). Alternatively, over-order and give your guests a fighting chance at falling over or yourself the guarantee of encouraging laughter for the duration of the speeches. Don't pour port if you want people to get up and boogie, as its effects can be soporific.

Wedding Anniversary

Time to have fun with vintages. Obviously, if you've only been married a year, there's not that much excitement in finding a year-old wine. But if it's your silver wedding anniversary and you've put up with each other for twenty-five long, hard years then you deserve to let loose and go wild on anything from rich and spicy vintage ports, treacly rich Madeira, Bordeaux reds or sweet whites, or a few cracking red Burgundies. (More on anniversary wines later in the book.)

If this is to be an intimate celebration my rough guidelines for Valentine's Day can be conveniently applied. Try to vary the formula a little from year to year to avoid being accused of being boringly predictable. Go all out on presentation. Serve with your finest linen and glasses, adhere to temperature control guides (especially if it's getting hot and steamy in the kitchen) and decant mature red wines in advance.

Baby

You've just given birth…probably the last thing you want, after feeling like you've done ten rounds with Lennox Lewis, is an alcoholic drink, let alone to be required to demonstrate hostessing skills to proud family members. Those around you will no doubt be showering you with fizz and flowers, but if you think you will want to say 'Cheers to Baby X!' at some point, then there's no harm in popping a few bottles of bubbly in the fridge at the same time as packing that overnight bag. Bubbly – predictable, but without equal to punctuate a celebration.

Christening

A religious occasion and thus not an obvious excuse for a right royal rave-up, but none the less a cause for celebration. Champagne might not be the prescribed match for christening cake but it should still go down perfectly well in all the excitement. It is, in fact, a complex flavour that's awkward to combine with most foods, but it is so special and delicious and the bubbles so distracting that it never really matters. For this I think you can be pretty sparing: just a glass or two a head. Sherry as well, both sweet (chilled) and dry (very chilled), is ideal for all the guests (except perhaps the anointed).

Lunch Party

Typically a lightweight meal affair and thus best matched with a light-alcohol white such as a German Riesling (which can be as low as 8 per cent), or a lightish-alcohol red (not usually much below 11.5 per cent). Keep plenty of water on hand if it's a weekday and you intend to go back to work, or the weekend and you want to do some shopping or lawn-mowing in the afternoon. If you are happy to have just one glass, it's a chilly day and you've got a rich dish in front of you, then why not have something a bit feistier to drink, such as an Australian Chardonnay or a Californian Cabernet.

A Sunday Roast

A family-uniting tradition or a good excuse to while away a Sunday in a boozy haze with your friends, hoping that tomorrow (Monday) never comes? Although the basic concept is fairly straightforward – i.e. meat and two or three veg – the final result, after hours of mingling flavours and juices, is often rich and complex. Of course, it depends what meat you are roasting and who you are trying to please or impress, but I think this respect-deserving feast should be accompanied by suitably serious wines, purse permitting. Remember roast flavours go well with smoky, oaky types. My suggestion for chicken, pork or turkey is white or red Burgundy, or Chardonnay or Pinot Noir from anywhere else in the world. For duck, it's got to be red Burgundy. There is no real need to decant a red Burgundy as it is unlikely to have much sediment and older versions may not hold up well to too much air exposure. A really top-class red Burgundy may well deserve the decanter treatment, however. For lamb, beef or game, dense and dark or peppery and spicy wines (see Chapter One) can compete well. These should definitely be decanted, not only to get them 'expressing themselves', but also because if you have invited friends to join you and made a big effort with the food, then it's worth making a ceremony of serving from an elegant decanter, if you've got one. If you haven't got anything snazzy, a simple jug will do. Decanting an hour before eating is good timing, unless the wines are very old and fragile. For all these wines, you want big-bowled glasses, to allow heavy-duty swirling and sniffing.

Tea Party

Funny time for wine? For dry wine certainly, but a drop of sweet sherry or grapey-scented Moscato is a very tempting teammate for scones, fruit cake and chocolate gâteaux. So put your teacup down and pick up a glass of one of these instead. Remember an hour or so in the fridge should set these sweet seducers up to satisfy.

Supper Party and Dinner Party

There's a big difference between a supper party and a dinner party in terms of the hostess's relationship to the wine. A supper party is a relaxed 'bung the booze on the table and help yourself' affair, whereas the formal element of a dinner party (i.e. you've had your hair done and painstakingly pre-planned the menu) requires a certain increased level of respect for the wines. It's time for the linen tablecloth, crystal glasses, matching napkins and the decanter. This is not to say you have to spend a fortune on any of it, but just that if you've got good food (no doubt more than one course), then it's worth finding wines capable of complementing your culinary contributions and serving them in peak condition. Persuade the uninitiated or unworldly among your guests to give fresh and lively Fino sherry a go with their nibbles. This should keep them distracted while you frantically finish laying the table. It's guaranteed to whet their appetites as well, so they'll be prepared to eat whatever you serve, even if it's a disaster. As ever, the wine choice is food dependent, but a fruity or aromatic white should please most palates (from the New World, it should be pungent and punchy), followed by a classic Rhône or Bordeaux red, unless you are having a creamy dish. From the style guide in Chapter One pick a sweet surprise for the end of the meal, either a sweet fortified, something golden and honeyed, or sweetness and light, depending on the final offer. If you are serving cheese then consider the texture, creaminess and strength of it, and have the choice of Bordeaux for the harder cheeses, a sweet white or fortified for the blue (Stilton) and the starter white for the rest. Full yet?

Late-night Drinking Session

I always keep a bottle or two of wine in the fridge in case I should be booze-enthusiastic enough while on an evening out to make that fateful suggestion, 'Hey, let's all pile back to mine and keep on drinking!' At which point, should we actually make it there, red wine usually calls out in the louder voice, 'Drink me!' So forget the stuff in the fridge and go for something medium and mellow, like a Merlot. Port always takes the rap for giving the worst hangovers, and as a fortified wine, with alcohol levels at 17 per cent plus, this is not surprising. However, it's more because it gets drunk at the end of a long night of indulgence that it's classified as a headache administrator. Be warned and drink it earlier in the day (breakfast not included).

Picnic in the Park

Picnics are preferably experienced in warm weather, although in the UK there's no guarantee of that. Think optimistically and plan white wines, which will need packing in iceboxes to get there. I'd be tempted to throw in a bottle of something bubbly to go with nibbles: a New World sparkling wine will do just as well as, if not better than, an inexpensive, possibly overacidic Champagne. A more sensible choice, gentler on the head and tongue, especially if you're picknicking in the afternoon or going to a lakeside concert that starts early evening, is the lightly sparkling Italian offerings of Prosecco or Asti. It's worth looking for some lighter-alcohol still whites, too. Try inexpensive (generally)

Muscadet, German Riesling, Pinot Grigio or other Italian whites, all of which are good for salads and light, cold food. Rosé works well for an event like this because it will go with the meat and tomato-based dishes you may well have in your hamper. This is an ideal opportunity for a drop of dessert wine too, to round off your rug picnic. Its sweetness and acidity create a perfectly pitched duet with fruit and fruity puddings. Plastic cups or even plastic wineglasses are the safest option, although it is smarter to take proper glasses as long as you wrap them up well in napkins.

Easter

See Sunday Roast for suggestions for the main meal and then think sticky (dessert wine) for the teatime intemperance of chocolate eggs and bunnies, simnel cake and hot cross buns. I love Easter. Asti Spumante (the light, grapey fizz from Italy) and Moscato are surprisingly good with chocolate, as are Tawny port, liqueur Muscat, Tokaji from Hungary and Mavrodaphne from Greece. Raisiny stickies such as sherry or port are a must match for dried fruit cakes or buns. So sit back, enjoy them and wait for the guilt to set in.

Christmas

My granny starts buying for Christmas in July, which I always find a little excessive. However, as ever, it's worth being well prepared. Decide what wines you want and order them well in advance. It's too frustrating to find they've sold out, or you can't get the quantities you want or find anywhere open at the last minute. 'A well-stocked cellar makes for a jolly Christmas' as the old adage, the one I invented, goes. Christmas is a time for classics, when traditional food demands the flavours of Burgundy, Bordeaux and the Rhône, not forgetting plenty of sparkling wine or Champoo. If you are all-day drinking, ease up on the alcohol a bit by refreshing your palate with a light and citrussy Mosel Riesling. Roast turkey and its trimmings need oaky whites so there's a good excuse to crack open some rich Chardonnays from Australia and California as well. Cheese asks more for red and nuts cry out for port. Christmas pudding in all its dried fruit and brandy-blazing glory begs for a sticky black Pedro Ximenez sherry, a marmaladey Tokaji or a molasses-thick Liqueur Muscat. It's time for decanting, too, so you can savour the flavours of older reds and ports. I insist, however, that port, like a puppy, should be for life, not just for Christmas.

New Year

Pop! Need I say more? Just remember to keep it chilled up to the last minute, have your flutes on standby, and when opening the bottle, aim away from eyes or panes of glass and twist the bottle base *not* the cork. Push down slightly on the cork as you do so, so it doesn't fly off out of your hand, and ease it out until you hear the 'sigh of a contented woman' (apparently). Now pour and have yourselves a very Happy New Year.

CHAPTER FIVE

Shopping

YOU PEER AHEAD AND AS FAR AS THE EYE CAN SEE IT ALL LOOKS the same. It's like a tunnel and it narrows at the end, but where it leads to you can't make out. To either side of you are turnings, and they all look the same too. Your heart starts beating faster and faster. You know you have got to get through here and get away. But how, and what do you take with you? Will you make a mistake and regret it later? Will it be too late to change your mind? Worse still ... will you have to come here again?

Does that sound familiar – a panic-struck, brain-befuddled visit to the wine aisles of a supermarket or off-licence? Most wine stockists these days do try to make it as straightforward as possible for us: dividing wines up by colour and country and arranging them clearly by price. They also display promotion or 'special offer' wines at the ends of aisles, so you can grab and run if you've got a plane to catch or a nuclear missile to intercept.

But when you don't have shopping bags of spare time to read all the flouncy, flowery descriptions on shelf-talkers or the backs of bottles, and you just want a decent, good value, uncomplicated, won't-answer-back bottle (or case) of wine to bung in the bottom of your trolley so that you can get to the cheese counter before it closes, then you probably grab what you know. You grab what you had last time and the time before that and the time before that. In fact, it's practically the only wine you ever buy and you can't remember its name or what country it comes from, but you could spot it anywhere because it's the one with the attractive 'sunset over a mountain range' label design.

And what is wrong with that? Producers and promoters of wine are fully aware that we women (and many men, too, though the heterosexual ones would never admit it) are swayed by the appearance of a bottle of wine. I, for one, chose my computer for the way it looked and will no doubt choose my next car according to what I can get in silver (my favourite car colour) at the time. Presentation matters to me and I am not ashamed to say that there is such a thing as a nice-looking bottle of wine.

So what happens when you go into a shop and are magnetically drawn to a wine bottle by its smooth and seductive frame, its up-to-the-minute, fashion-conscious appearance, and its bold, striking words? You get up close and personal to it, and then you realize you've no idea what the message on the bottle is all about.

What do *Appellation Contrôlée* or *embotellado en la propiedad* mean? What's that percentage on the label, and what's that date for? Not only do we have to contend with a monumental choice of wine but we've also got to be fluent in the language of at least thirty different wine-growing countries, as well as understand their law-unto-themselves labelling systems.

Message on a Bottle

A wine label is not just an excuse for a pretty picture and exercising a fancy font. It is the wine's passport, helping you to identify it and work out whether you think it should have been allowed into the country in the first place. (Some of the most exciting wines I have ever tasted came from mould-encased flagons labelled with the vague remains of decayed and unreadable etchings, but that's another story.) Here are some of the words you are most likely to come across, and what they tell you about the wine.

The Bottom Rung: Table Wine

Vin de Table (France), Vino da Tavola (Italy), Vino/Vinho de Mesa (Spain/Portugal), Deutscher Tafelwein (Germany) = Table Wine, the bottom rung of the quality ladder. Flush it, or most of it at least. Or serve it at the end of the night when all the good stuff has gone and nobody cares any more.

The Middle Rung: Country Wine

Vin de Pays (France), Indicazione Geografica Tipica – IGT (Italy), Vino/Vinho de la Tierra (Spain/Portugal), Qualitätswein bestimmter Anbaugebiete – QbA (Germany) = Country wine/middle level, where much of the volume is and many of the bargains are.

The Top Rung

Appellation (name of region) Contrôlée – AC (France), Denominazione di Origine Controllata/Garantita – DOC/G (Italy), Denominacíon de Origen – DO (Spain), Qualitätswein mit Prädikat – QmP (Germany) = top-rung-of-quality-ladder wines from a specific region. The wines are supposed to display the character of that region and have been made in accordance with rules of the region (apparently).

Producer-bottled

Mis en bouteille à la propriété/au domaine (French), Imbottigliato al origine (Italian), Embotellado en la propiedad (Spain), Original/Erzeuger abfüllung (German), Estate bottled = bottled by the producer. Preferable to transported somewhere else for bottling – risks of oxidation, temperature variation and bad traffic – although shipping in bulk can make for bargains.

Cru

In French wines, a *cru* (or growth, as it is also termed) indicates a wine estate, vineyard or château. Premier/1er Cru and, superior still, Grand Cru are those highest in the ranks. In the Médoc in Bordeaux, there is a more complex and confusing five *cru* quality assessment system.

Percentage

This reveals what percentage of the wine, by volume, is alcohol, such as '13% vol'.

Year/Vintage

The year is that in which the grapes were picked (harvested) to make the wine. 'NV' on a wine, or the absence of a date, means it was made with a blend of juice from more than one year. Vintage Champagne uses the grapes from just one year, and is only made when the grapes are considered good enough (the same applies to vintage port).

Traditional Method

Traditional Method, Méthode Traditionelle, Méthode Classique, Metodo Tradizionale/Classico, Méthode Cap Classique – all indicate a sparkling wine that has been made in the same way as Champagne, undergoing a secondary fermentation in bottle.

Old Vines

'Vieilles Vignes' means the wine has been made with grapes that come from old vines. There are no real rules as to when they qualify for being 'old' (a bit like us gals, really), so the term can be misleading. The suggestion, however, is that the juice from these grapes will have more concentration and flavour.

Reserve

This often means nothing at all (though see Reserva, in Spain, page 124). It *can* mean a more full-flavoured wine made with better grapes that have spent longer in oak, but it's just as likely to mean nothing and have been plonked on the label to impress the unsuspecting.

Supérieur/Superiore

Means the wine has a higher alcohol content and has probably been aged for longer, but not necessarily that it is superior. Though it might be.

'Sweet or dry, madam?'

In France

Brut	usually on fizz, means dry
Demi-sec	medium-dry
Moelleux	usually on Vouvray, means sweet
Liquoreux	super sweet

In Italy/Spain

Secco/Seco	dry
Dolce/Dulce	sweet

In Germany

Trocken	dry
Halbtrocken	medium-dry
Lieblich/süss	very sweet

Identities

All wines carry the producers' name somewhere, anything from a fat-cat Californian company, to a tiny producer from Croatia, all twelve sons and the names of his dogs. Wines are also identified by region and/or grape, as well as other country-specific factors. Here is a quick country guide.

France

You will see, especially in Bordeaux and Burgundy, a Château or Domaine name, such as Château Tour de Mirambeau, or else a brand name such as Moûton-Cadet, Le Piat d'Or, Fat Bastard. Appellation Contrôlée wines are not traditionally labelled with the grape variety but instead with a geographical name: the AC region (as they are in Italy: DOC/G region; and Spain: DO region). For example, Sancerre is a delimited region, as is Chablis, Chianti in Italy and Rioja in Spain. These regional wines may be made of one variety of grape or a blend of different ones. Alsace is an exception because of its Germanic connection: their wines carry the grape variety on the label. Vin de Pays wines have the grape variety on the label as well as the particular, often very broad Vin de Pays area from which the grapes were sourced – Vin de Pays d'Oc is the most common.

Germany

There will be the name of the village (such as Brauneberger) where the vines were planted and the name of the vineyard (such as Juffer Sonnenuhr) where the grapes came from, then the grape variety (such as Riesling), then the style of the wine (defined by the level of ripeness of the grapes), as follows:

Kabinett – normal harvesting, lighter style, usually quite dry.

Spätlese – means late-picked, so the grapes were very ripe. More intensity of flavour and more sweetness can be expected.

Auslese – means individually picked bunches, picked for their ripeness, thus offering even more flavour and sweetness.

Beerenauslese – each grape berry is hand-chosen and picked, typically for the 'noble rot' (botrytis) that has concentrated its sugars; very sweet, honeyed wines.

Trockenbeerenauslese – each *dry* grape berry, shrivelled by 'noble rot', is picked by hand. The sweetest and rarest of all the styles, expensive and exquisite, like a special syrup.

Eiswein – 'ice wine', made from grapes frozen on the vine. They are pressed when frozen so there is very little water, only sugar and acidity. Nectar in a glass. (It's cold enough in Canada that they can make it there too.)

Italy

In DOCG and DOC wines the label will name a specific geographical sub-region or village or town where certain grapes are permitted, such as Soave (Garganega grape) or Valpolicella (Corvina and other grapes), or a grape variety attached to a region, such as Barbera (grape) d'Asti (region). In IGT wines you'll see the grape variety and the broader geographical region, such as Puglia or Toscana.

Spain

On DO wines, you'll find the region and perhaps a wine name as well, such as Viña Sol, or a winery, such as Viña Albali. There will often be a wine style category as well, indicating how long the wine has spent in oak barrels:

Crianza – minimum two years' ageing (one in barrel, one in bottle)
Reserva – minimum three years' ageing (one in barrel, two in bottle)
Gran Reserva – minimum five years' ageing (two in barrel, three in bottle)

Spain is home to sherry, from the region of Jerez, and there is a language for the different styles of this as well:

Fino – dry style, light and fresh
Manzanilla – also dry style, but with salty tang too
Amontillado – Fino aged in oak barrels, brown and nutty, sometimes slightly sweet

Palo Cortado – a dry Amontillado, aged to develop richness more like that of Oloroso
Oloroso – long-aged sherry, more alcohol and colour, can be slightly sweet or dry
Cream – sweetened Oloroso made for export to Britain, that is, to us sweet-toothed suckers
PX – sweetest style of all, made from the super-ripe Pedro Ximenez grape: it's like molasses. It's sinful.

Note that sherry can only come from its demarcated region of Jerez in Spain. Fortified wine like this made anywhere else can only be called sherry-style. See also port, below, and it's the same with Champagne, of course.

Portugal

On DO wines the label will name a Quinta (the vineyard estate) and perhaps a grape variety, such as Touriga Nacional, as well as, of course, the DO region.

Portugal is home to port, from the Douro region, and there is a label vocabulary to describe the different styles of this as well:

White port – as it says, and best served with tonic water, ice and a slice as Portonic. Keep it chilled.
Ruby port – a blend of wines from different years, in tank or barrel for two years on average and in the bottle for no time at all before release into the big, wide market. Basic stuff. Some producers make a Premium Ruby, which is a bit better.
Tawny port – a blend of wines from different years aged in barrels for a long time. Brown, nutty, sweet and irresistible. Colheitas are Tawny ports but from a single year.
Vintage Character port – these are blends that have spent four to six years in barrels. They are at the cheaper and simpler end of the scale.
Late Bottled Vintage port, or LBV – these are ports made every year from a single year's grapes (see Vintage

port), aged in barrel for four years. Filtered, so, unlike Vintage Port, don't need decanting.

Vintage port – these are ports made only in years that are declared great and only from top vineyard sites, namely those best positioned for producing the finest fruit (unlike LBV). Aged for only two years in barrel and then forever in bottle (or until you can't wait any longer). Not filtered.

Crusted port – made in the style of Vintage, that is, two years in barrel and non-filtered, but from a blend of wines from more than one year.

Single Quinta Vintage port – these are made with grapes from one vineyard estate, not usually in a declared vintage year, but in a year where that site is great enough to produce a vintage on its own. In Vintage years these grapes would go into making Vintage port instead.

Note that port comes only from the Douro region of Portugal. A similar fortified wine made anywhere else can only be called port-style.

New World

This refers to the USA, South Africa, Chile, Argentina, Australia and New Zealand. The label will have the grape variety (nearly always), the region the grapes are from, and sometimes a name for the wine that could be inspired by anything from a local site of great historical value, a beautiful view or the name of the producer's recently departed budgie.

Each of these countries has or is developing its own demarcation system for appellation labelling, though the rules surrounding the origins of the grapes are much more lenient in the New World than the Old. Grapes (or juice) can be transported great distances from where they were picked to where they will be blended at the winery. The bottle can be labelled with a particular variety even if there are small percentages (up to 15 per cent usually) of other varieties in there too.

Other Countries

Note that Greece and most of Eastern Europe usually put the variety or varieties on the label. Greek grape variety names, in particular, will challenge most with their sheer unpronounceability. Look out also for a region and the producer's name.

Misconceptions

Appearances can put you *off* a purchase, and there are times when prejudices or preconceptions could get in the way of you having a darn good time with a darn fine wine. So here are some fallacies laid to rest.

A screw cap on a bottle doesn't necessarily mean the wine is cheap and nasty. In 2000, sixteen top Riesling producers in the Clare Valley, Australia took the plunge and sealed their premium Rieslings (some worth £15 a bottle or more) with Stelvin screw caps in order to prove that it is the most effective way to keep wines fresh for longer and to prevent them from being 'corked'. Since then others around the world have followed suit, encouraging people to see that screw caps can be used on expensive wine to very positive effect. The only things preventing screw caps from becoming more widespread are deep-set prejudice and a lasting love affair with the tradition of cork-pulling.

A long, tapered, green flute bottle with foreign writing on it isn't necessarily German. Alsace uses the same bottle shape and the wines inside are rather different to German wines: they tend to have more concentration and more alcohol, although they may be made with the same aromatic grapes, such as Riesling. And, anyway, not all German wines taste like Liebfraumilch. The idea that all German wines are unappealing is a most unfortunate delusion to labour under. There, that's two misconceptions dealt with in one.

Just because a bottle says 'sherry' on the label doesn't

mean it is sickly sweet and meant only for the aged. Fino and Manzanilla sherries are dry, mouth-watering and perfect as appetite-whetting, chilled aperitifs with olives, salted almonds or anything under the title of tapas. You can get more layers of flavour for your money with sherry than with any other wine on the market. I simply cannot say this about sherry often enough!

Just because a bottle says 'port' on the label doesn't mean you must only drink it at the end of Christmas dinner with Stilton, guaranteeing a Boxing Day hangover. Port in all styles, chilled, can make a scrumptious aperitif at any time of the day or year, especially if you serve it with nuts. So long as it is not the last thing you drink at night, it is unlikely to be a cranium-crippler.

Tip: Vintage port and chocolate are wild bed partners.

Classic italic script on labels is often a big turn-on, especially for men. It spells 'tradition' and 'heritage' and shouts 'Respect me!' and, a bit louder, 'Buy me!' Don't be suckered by this and at the same time put off trying modern or trendy-looking stuff. Many quality cult wines, new releases and sought-after samples are dressed up to look flashy, modern and even gimmicky, when the wine inside is serious stuff – just as serious as anything under classic lettering.

Just because the bottle is heavy doesn't mean the wine inside is heavyweight. If a wine costing four or five pounds is in a stylish, thick glass bottle you ought to ask yourself how much money was saved on the wine in order to cover the costs of producing the bottle. Proceed with suspicion.

Making your choice

So, now you are no longer baffled by labels and you've been freed of a few misconceptions. You still need to make your own choices, however. Remember my style guide in Chapter One? This can be your first tactic. Once you've identified the styles of wine you particularly like, say, spicy and aromatic whites from the Rhône, then you can consider trying other wines within that style category, such as aromatic whites from Australia. These, in turn, might lead you to other styles and flavours you like.

Decision-making is made easier these days by the freedom we have to identify a wine by its grape variety. Both women and men are increasingly seeking out trusted and admired grape varieties, often making this choice over that of country of origin. (Having bought a wine previously still tends to come top in the list of decision-making factors, however.) Remember, though, that the choice of grape variety may well be down to the country the wine comes from, so that in some ways variety and country of origin are interdependent.

What makes choosing wine easier today than it was, say, twenty years ago in the heady days of Duran Duran, ra-ra skirts and pixie boots, is that although there was much less choice on the shelves then (countries like New Zealand and Argentina hadn't even entered the world wine game), in many ways the flavours were more varied. Player countries were producing wines from their native varieties in their own, often very individual way. Now, as technology and communications have developed, traditional regional tactics have been ousted by shared innovation and a universal method of attack, both in choice of varieties as well as winemaking approaches. 'Flying winemakers' jet round the world rolling their winemaking dice in as many different countries as they can comfortably manage in a year. Winemakers now exchange the 'international grape variety' cards, those varieties that the French insist, and rightly, were theirs in the first place, such as Cabernet Sauvignon, Chardonnay, Syrah (Shiraz), Merlot and Sauvignon Blanc. If you can find the same grape variety from Alsace to Australia, made by the same energetic aerodynamic oenologist, the chances are there will be considerable similarities. So if you like one, you'll like the lot.

What's more, we, the consumers, with our style preferences and flavour favouring, also dictate to a certain extent the decreasing choice we now have in the shops. As our buying trends are reported back into the industry, wines are made-to-order for us at the request of supermarket and off-licence buyers. Styles and flavours are becoming increasingly homogenized to suit consumer cravings, and created on demand in any country around the world.

There might be a cold-sweat-inducing array of differently shaped, sized, coloured and labelled bottles standing proudly on our shop shelves these days, but in truth the flavours inside are becoming more and more the same. This might ease some of our purchasing panic but sadly it also reduces our range of taste experiences.

A way through the maze

When shopping for wine, go armed with an idea of what you want the wine for. Is it to go with a particular culinary creation, or just to have in the fridge should the fancy take you? Is it to impress an ostentatious drinking partner, or for glugging with a gang of friends? Do you want a quick fix of easy-drinking pleasure or complex and contemplative imbibing?

Another way to help yourself is to find a reliable and trustworthy (local if possible) wine merchant or supplier with whom you can build a good relationship. You want one who will take your hand in his and guide you as you wander along the long and winding road of wine choices, and whose advice you are prepared to listen to (in other words, you are not afraid he is trying to palm off his difficult-to-sell wines on you). He, or indeed she, should be prepared to suggest unusual and exciting wines that satisfy your experimental hunger, and able to understand your aversions so that you won't be disappointed with what you take home.

Certain wines demand more of you than others. One reason to give a wine consideration is when you've spent the best part of a week's wages on it, so equip yourself as well with an idea of how much you want to/are able to spend before you go.

Cost Guide

To what extent is price an indication of quality? The difference in quality between a £4 wine and a £14 wine (of comparable styles) should be detectable by the merest mortal regardless of tasting experience. The more expensive wine will have more richness of flavour, different levels of flavour and probably more colour. This will have been achieved through the use of better quality, selected grapes and more time and care in the winery, which should include processes that develop the wine's complexity and assist its ageing potential.

This may also be true of a £140 wine and a £1,400 wine, but what is more true of these wines is that their rarity or limited availability plus demand equals rarefied prices.

Here is a guide to retail wine prices and what you can expect to get for your money.

£2.50 to £4

Supermarket specialization. Weedy wines from Old World and jammy ones from the New. Most oak is flavouring from wood chips soaked in the wine, because this price doesn't allow for leaving the wine in oak barrels. These wines sometimes give the impression that you are going to get lots of flavour, but it's gone in an instant. These guys don't hang around. They are heartbreakers. Much of this is stuff I wouldn't even cook with, made from grapes I certainly wouldn't eat. From £3.50 upwards you can find bargains with a bit more flavour. They will be soft and easy, most of them, but won't offer any genuine oral excitement.

£4 to £7

More flavour and concentration. You can start to feel comfortable taking them round to people's houses for dinner and introducing them to your friends. These are wines that stand up to food rather than just helping to wash it down. The oak flavour (if applicable) is likely to come from barrels, not chips. These wines hang around at the end of the mouthful but probably not at the end of the night – they give you a reminder on the finish of what came before (in other words, they have a bit of length).

£7 to £10

Of more interest still, here we have wines with good structure and balance, and a lingering aftertaste. These wines will be made more lovingly with quality oak barrels (if applicable), using better quality grapes. Their flavour will last in your mouth long after swallowing. You'll want to have another date with these fellas, and why not? These are wines you could even introduce to your parents.

£10 to £40

Big wines packed with layers of flavour and a balance of fruit with acidity and tannin (in reds). These wines are built to last; they are the marrying kind. If they seem too boisterous when they are young they will definitely reward you in maturity. Not all are for jumping into bed with straight away. Spend time with them first.

£40 and above

Wines for worshipping not drinking! Wines for investing in or giving as gifts to those you want to fall in love with you. These wines will have super concentrated flavour, balance, and length to make you weep. They will have been handcrafted from only the best, most carefully selected grapes, and dutifully watched over in the winery where they might have spent a good few years being caressed by the loving touch of oak. If this is not the case, you've been had. As with the £10 to £40 wines, these might need time to truly open up and express themselves.

Supermarket Secrets ...

...and high-street stores' hidden depths. Most supermarkets and off-licences stock a wide range of wines from around the world to meet the demands of the many and varied shoppers of the British Isles. More than 60 per cent of all wine sold is through them, amounting to about 42 million cases a year. This means the buyers go to large suppliers with brand-scale quantities. Some stockists specialize in particular regions or countries where they think they can offer real value for money (while making a bob or two themselves, of course). Here is a list of supermarkets and high-street chains and the wines, styles, varieties, countries and obscurities I think they excel at. If any of these areas gets you going, there's contact information for you to seek out more of what you fancy.

Please note that in these competitive times the retail market is highly susceptible to change. The following information was accurate on going to print, but with acquisitions and consolidations in the pipeline, changes will no doubt have happened since. A year from now the situation may be different again.

Aldi

Very short list (thirty wines) and very cheap too (maximum selling price for still wines of £4.99) but some of them are surprisingly drinkable.

Tel 08705 134 262

Website www.aldi-stores.co.uk

Asda

South America, Spain, France, especially Bordeaux. Cheapies and brands, with some new stuff of interest.

Tel 0113 241 9172

Fax 0113 241 7766

Website www.asda.co.uk

Booths

France, especially Bordeaux and Burgundy, Spain, Portugal, sweet wines and fortifieds. The Waitrose of the north for quality and interest. Visit www.everywine.co.uk for the range.

Tel 0800 072 0011

Fax 01772 329 700

Website www.booths-supermarkets.co.uk

Co-op

South America, South Africa, Australia, vegetarian/vegan. Choice at the cheap end.

Tel 0845 090 2222

Co-op Drink Online

E-mail customer.services@co-op2u.com

Website www.co-op2u.co.uk

'First Quench' Chain…

…includes: Thresher Wine Shop, Victoria Wine, Wine Rack, Bottoms Up. Champagne, New Zealand, Australia, Bordeaux, Chile. Good, imaginative list, especially £5 and above.

Tel 01707 387 200

Fax 01707 387 416

Website www.enjoyment.co.uk

Majestic

Germany, rosé. Many wines here I'd like a case of. Sold only by case.

Tel 01923 298 226

Fax 01923 819 105

E-mail info@majestic.co.uk

Website www.majestic.co.uk

Marks and Spencer

Rhône, Loire, southern France, Australia, Germany. Getting better every year.

Tel 020 7935 4422
Fax 020 7268 2674
Website www.marksandspencer.com

Morrisons

Pretty predictable but well priced.

Tel 01924 870 000
Fax 01924 872 250
Website www.morereasons.co.uk

Nicolas UK

France, not surprisingly since it's a French company. In particular, Bordeaux, Rhône and sparkling wines.

Tel 020 8964 5469
Fax 020 8962 9829
Website www.nicolas-wines.com

Oddbins

Greece, Bordeaux, Australia. Most consistently interesting and broad-reaching quality choices on the high street.

Tel 0800 328 2323
Fax 0800 328 3848
E-mail customer.services@oddbinsmail.com
Website www.oddbins.com

Safeway

Australia, Vin de Pays, Bordeaux, Eastern Europe. Some good cheapies but mainly predictable brands at the higher end. In-store wine sales only.

Tel 020 8970 3821
Fax 020 8756 2910
Website www.safeway.co.uk

Sainsbury's

Bordeaux, southern France, North Africa, Chile, Kosher wines, Italy, wine boxes. Obvious but wide-reaching choices. Boosts 'Babe' Chardonnay 'for the girl that wants it all'.

Tel 0800 636 262
Fax 020 7695 7610
Website www.sainsbury's.co.uk

Somerfield...

...including Kwik Save. Italy, southern France, Chile. Showing increasing originality and thought.

Tel 0117 935 9359

Fax 0117 978 0629

Website www.somerfield.co.uk

Tesco

Organic wines, Australia, 'Finest' range (like their 'Finest' range of foods). Largest wine retailer in the country with over 8,000 wines in the range.

Tel 0800 505 555

E-mail customer.service@tesco.co.uk

Website www.tesco.com

Unwins

Italy, Loire, South Africa, Bordeaux. Mix of predictable and original.

Tel 01322 272 711

Fax 01322 294 469

E-mail info@unwins.co.uk

Website www.unwins.co.uk

Waitrose

Fine wines (Inner Cellar), Bordeaux, Europe in general, Germany, Australia, South Africa. Best overall supermarket range by a country mile.

Wines Direct

Tel 0800 188 881

E-mail winedirect@waitrose.co.uk

Waitrose Fine Wines

Tel 01344 825 929

Fax 01344 825 926

E-mail finewine@waitrose.co.uk

Website www.waitrosedirect.co.uk

Specialists

Of course, our humble islands are dotted with small local wine merchants who often seek out rarer or lesser-known wines or focus specifically on particular country, regional or remote-hilly-village personal passions. These are at the top of the charts for certain categories.

English Wine Centre

As its name suggests.
Alfriston Roundabout, East Sussex BN26 5QS
Tel 01323 870 164
Fax 01323 870 005
E-mail bottles@englishwine.co.uk
Website www.englishwine.co.uk

Falcon Vintners

Italophiles.
74 Warren Street, London W1P 5PA
Tel 020 7388 7055
E-mail eric@falconvintners.co.uk

For the Love of Wine

Italian and Swiss enthusiasts.
Flint Cottage, High Rougham, Bury St Edmunds, Suffolk IP30 9LN
Tel 01280 822 500
Fax 01280 823 833
E-mail mail@i-love-wine.co.uk
Website www.i-love-wine.co.uk

Justerini and Brooks

Rhône maniacs; Burgundy and Germany serious too.
Office 61 St James's Street, London SW1A 1LZ
Tel 020 7484 6400
Fax 020 7484 6499

Laymont and Shaw

Spain fame, and e-commerce too.
The Old Chapel, Milpool, Truro, Cornwall TR1 1EX
Tel 01872 270 545
Fax 01872 223 005
E-mail sales@spanish-wine-specialists.co.uk
Website www.laymont-shaw.co.uk

Moreno Wine Merchants

Spain again.
11 Marylands Road, London W9 2DU
Tel 020 7286 0678
Fax 020 7286 0513
E-mail morenowi@dialstart.net
Website www.moreno-winedirect.com

Philglass and Swiggott

New World champions and my top shop name!
21 Northcote Road, London SW11 1NG
Tel 020 7924 4494
Fax 020 7924 4736
E-mail philandswig@aol.com

Roberson

Champagne conquerors and lots of expensive stuff.
348 Kensington High Street, London W14 8NS
Tel 020 7371 2121
Fax 020 7371 4010
E-mail cliff@roberson.co.uk
Website www.roberson.co.uk

Sommelier Wine Company

Fine wines and rosés unrivalled.
23 St George's Esplanade, St Peter Port, Guernsey GY1 2BG
Tel 01481 721 677
Fax 01481 716 818

Tanners Wines

German gurus, and e-commerce too.
26 Wyle Cop, Shrewsbury, Shropshire SY1 1XD
Tel 01743 234 455
Fax 01743 234 501
E-mail sales@tanners-wines.co.uk
Website www.tanners-wines.co.uk

Valvona and Crolla Ltd

Italophiles, and e-commerce too.
19 Elm Row, Edinburgh EH7 4AA
Tel 0131 556 6066
Fax 0131 556 1668
E-mail wine@valvonacrolla.co.uk
Website www.valvonacrolla.co.uk

Vin du Van Wine Merchants

Australian artistes.
Colthups, The Street, Appledore, Kent TN26 2BX
Tel 01233 758 727
Fax 01233 758 389

Peter Wylie Fine Wines

King of older vintages; e-commerce too.

Plymtree Manor, Plymtree, Cullompton, Devon EX15 2LE
Tel 01884 277 555
Fax 01884 277 557
E-mail peter@wylie-fine-wines.demon.co.uk
Website www.wyliefinewines.co.uk

Yapp Brothers

Rhône and Loire stars; e-commerce too.

The Old Brewery, Mere, Wiltshire BA12 6DY
Tel 01747 860 423
Fax 01747 860 929
E-mail sales@yapp.co.uk
Website www.yapp.co.uk

The Big O

The environmentally conscious or concerned among you and indeed even the most unobservant will be well aware by now of the firmly established trend for organic wines (and food in general). These are made with grapes farmed without pesticides, herbicides, fungicides or chemical fertilizers, and in accordance with the rules of official accreditation bodies (rules that apply both in the vineyard and in the winery). Lower levels of the preservative sulphur dioxide are used, which can help allergy sufferers (reducing nasty reactions like asthma, migraines, breathing problems and skin rashes that make you look permanently embarrassed). Hangovers should also be reduced as a result of fewer additives, but that still depends more on how much wine you get through and whether you are being fed and watered at the same time. Biodynamic producers take their principles a step further, studying the alignment of the planets and the movement of the moon in order to understand plant growth and make wine with minimum intervention or harmful effects on the environment.

Not all organic producers declare it on the label, and if they do it may be in a foreign tongue. Look for *biologique* (French), *biologica* (Italian), *ökologische* (German) and *ecologico* (Spanish), and the details of the certifying body. In the UK it's the Soil Association. Organic and biodynamic specialists follow.

Adnams

Strong organic/biodynamic selection, as well as being thoroughly impressive all-rounders with e-commerce and mail order and a shop.

Sole Bay Brewery, East Green, Southwold, Suffolk IP18 6JW
Tel 01502 727 200
Fax 01502 727 201
E-mail wines@adnams.co.uk
Website www.adnams.co.uk

The Organic Wine Company

Good long list, especially covering France and Italy. E-commerce too.

PO Box 81, High Wycombe, Buckinghamshire HP13 5QN
Tel 01494 446 557
Fax 01494 446 557
E-mail info@organicwinecompany.com
Website www.organicwinecompany.com

The Purewine Company

Small set-up, limited range. E-commerce too.

Ocean House, 51 Alcantra House, Ocean Village, Southampton SO14 3HR
Tel 023 8023 8214
E-mail contact@purewine.co.uk
Website www.purewine.co.uk

Smithfield Wines

Organic and vegetarian wines mail order and over the net.

Unit 14, Carioca Business Park, 2 Heldon Close, Manchester M12 4AH
Tel 0161 273 6070
Fax 0161 273 6090
E-mail sales@smithfieldwine.com
Website www.smithfieldwine.com

Vintage Roots

Interesting range, in particular France, Spain and Italy. E-commerce too.

Farley Farms, Reading Road, Arborfield, Berkshire RG2 9HT
Tel 0800 980 4992
Fax 0118 976 1998
E-mail info@vintageroots.co.uk
Website www.vintageroots.co.uk

Vinceremos

The most extensive list of the lot. E-commerce too.
74 Kirkgate, Leeds LS2 7DJ
Tel 0113 244 0002
Fax 0113 288 4566
E-mail info@vinceremos.co.uk
Website www.vinceremos.co.uk

Vegetarian Concerns

You don't have to go to a specialist merchant to find wines that show the necessary respect to living things that vegetarians or vegans request. An increasing number of wines are meeting vegetarian and vegan demands. Look on the back labels to see for yourself (although sadly some wines that are vegetarian don't state it). You can be pretty confident when buying organic that the wine will be vegetarian or vegan as well.

If you are scratching your head over where the pork chop is in an alcoholic drink made from grape juice, then I'll explain. Before being bottled a wine is clarified by a process called fining that removes leftover particles (of proteins, yeasts, etc) that would make the wine murky. Fining agents can be made from gelatine (pig or cow bones), isinglass (fish swim bladders) or egg white and milk protein. The alternative that keeps both vegetarians and vegans happy is a clay-based agent called bentonite.

For more information you can contact the Vegetarian Society: tel 0161 925 2000; e-mail info@vegsoc.org; website www.vegsoc.org.

Mail Order and E-commerce

If you are not keen on getting lost at sea on the shop floor or you don't get out much because you're imprisoned in your home by a screaming nappy-soiler – then mail order and e-commerce are for you. In most cases local delivery is free (minimum one case), but further afield usually brings about a charge. This is my pick of the bunch of *mail order and/or e-commerce only*, that is, they have no shop to browse in. I include, of course, which regions, countries, categories they are hottest in. This does mean, sadly, that you cannot pick up, feel and examine the bottles. (Oh – is that just me?)

A and B Vintners

Hot on Rhône, Burgundy and Languedoc-Roussillon.
Tel 01892 724 977
Fax 01892 722 673
E-mail info@abvintners.co.uk
Website www.abvintners.co.uk

John Armit Wines

Free nationwide delivery. Hot on Bordeaux, Burgundy and Italy.
Tel 020 7908 0600
Fax 020 7908 0601
E-mail info@armit.co.uk
Website www.armit.co.uk

Australian Wine Club

Hot on what it suggests.
Tel 0800 856 2004
Fax 020 8843 8444
E-mail orders@austwine.co.uk
Website www.austwine.co.uk

Andrew Chapman Fine Wines

Hot on Australia and France.
Tel 01235 550 707
Fax 0870 136 6335
E-mail info@surf4wine.co.uk
Website www.surf4wine.co.uk

Domaine Direct

Hot on Burgundy, California and Australian.
Tel 020 7837 1142
Fax 020 7837 8605
E-mail info@domainedirect.co.uk
Website www.domainedirect.co.uk

Farr Vintners

Scorching on Bordeaux.
Tel 020 7821 2000
Fax 020 7821 2020
E-mail sales@farr-vintners.com
Website www.farr-vintners.com

Fine and Rare Wines

Hot on what it says.
Tel 020 8960 1995
Fax 020 8960 1911
E-mail wine@frw.co.uk
Website www.frw.co.uk

Great Gaddesden Wines

Hot on unusuals, such as Greece, Austria, Mexico.
Tel 01582 760 606
Fax 01582 760 505
E-mail info@flyingcorkscrew.com

Great Grog

Young and funky New World from two ex-Oddbins chaps. Free nationwide delivery.
Tel 0131 662 4777
Fax 0131 662 4983
E-mail info@greatgrog.co.uk
Website www.greatgrog.co.uk

Roger Harris Wines

Beaujolais barmy.
Tel 01603 880 171
Fax 01603 880 291
E-mail sales@rogerharriswines.co.uk
Website www.beaujolaisonline.co.uk

Liberty Wines

Wholesalers who also sell direct to the public. Free nationwide delivery. Hot on Italy, Australia and Germany.
Tel 020 7720 5350
Fax 020 7720 6158
E-mail info@libertywine.co.uk
Website www.libertywines.co.uk

O.W. Loeb

Hot on Rhône, Burgundy and Germany.
Tel 020 7928 7750
Fax 020 7928 1855
E-mail sales@owloeb.com
Website www.owloeb.com

Morris and Verdin

Hot on Burgundy and California.
Tel 020 7921 5300
Fax 020 7921 5333
E-mail info@m-v.co.uk
Website www.morris-verdin.co.uk

New Zealand Wines Direct

Needs no explanation. Small set-up.
Tel 020 7482 0093
Fax 020 7267 8400
E-mail margaret.harvey@btinternet.com
Website www.fwnz.co.uk

Howard Ripley

Hot on Burgundy and Germany.
Tel 020 8877 3065
Fax 020 8877 0029
E-mail info@howardripley.com
Website www.howardripley.com

Swig

Hot on Rhône, Italy, South Africa.
Tel 020 7903 8311
Fax 020 7093 8313
E-mail imbibe@swig.co.uk
Website www.swig.co.uk

Wine Alive

Internet-based retailer. Good organic and 'fine and rare' sections.
Tel 0800 015 5960
Fax 0800 015 5961
E-mail info@winealive.co.uk
Website www.winealive.co.uk

Wine Society

Members-only cooperative. Very good on French and New World.
Tel 01438 741 177
Fax 01438 761 167
E-mail memberservices@thewinesociety.com
Website www.thewinesociety.com

Wine Treasury

Hot on California.
Tel 020 7793 9999
Fax 020 7793 8080
E-mail jdoidge@winetreasury.com
Website www.winetreasury.com

Wine Vault

Australian wine authority.

Tel 01622 631 862
E-mail sales@winevault.co.uk
Website www.winevault.co.uk

Surf and Shop

A most hassle-free way to get wine, as long as you've got fast internet access and your computer doesn't crash as often as mine, is to order it over the net and have it delivered when and wherever you want it. Competition is fierce for those who wish to stay afloat in the fickle ocean of the internet (a fair few original sites have gone under), so many now offer incentives such as 'don't pay if you don't like it' as well as whopping great discounts and special offers. The following are strong e-commerce websites (with no retail outlet) that also offer editorial content for the wine curious who want to expand their knowledge while emptying their wallets. Sites include articles from journalists, recommendations and general wine information.

Wine e-commerce sites with editorial content

www.virginwines.com
www.ItsWine.com
www.everywine.co.uk (this is Booths' selection online; see page 134)
www.ChateauOnline.co.uk
www.Bringmywine.com
www.Madaboutwine.com
www.wineandco.com

Pick of the Rest

Here's my pick of other merchants who offer excellent e-commerce but also have shops for the browser who likes a choice. There may be one near you.

Ballantyne's

Award-winning Welsh merchant.

3 Westgate, Cowbridge, Vale of Glamorgan CF71 7AQ
Tel 01446 774 840
Fax 01446 775 253
E-mail enq@ballantynes.co.uk
Website www.ballantynes.co.uk

Berry Bros and Rudd

This company is 300 years old. Top wines, especially from Bordeaux, Burgundy, Germany and the Rhône. Shop is a must-visit if you are in London; it's like a museum.

3 St James's Street, London SW1A 1EG
Tel 020 7396 9600
Fax 020 7396 9611
E-mail orders@bbr.com
Website www.bbr.co.uk

Bibendum

Strong all over but French is hottest.

113 Regent's Park Road, London NW1 8UR
Tel 020 7722 5577
Fax 020 7722 7354
E-mail sales@bibendum-wine.co.uk
Website www.bibendum-wine.co.uk

Chandos Deli

Italian enthusiasts.

6 Princess Victoria Street, Clifton, Bristol BS8 4BP
Tel 0117 974 3275
Fax 0117 973 1020
E-mail info@chandosdeli.com
Website www.chandosdeli.com

Cockburns of Leith

Historic, 200-year-old Edinburgh wine merchants.

7 Devon Place, Edinburgh EH12 5HJ
Tel 0131 346 1113
Fax 0131 313 2607
E-mail info@winelist.co.uk
Website www.winelist.co.uk

Corney and Barrow

Long-established fine wine merchant and broker. Brilliant wine bars.

Head Office: 12 Helmet Row, London EC1V 3TD
Tel 020 7539 3200
Fax 020 7608 1373
E-mail wine@corbar.co.uk
Website corneyandbarrow.com

Irma Fingal-Rock

Burgundy mad, with a lot more too. Love the name.
64 Monmow Street, Monmouth NP25 3EN
Tel/Fax 01600 712 372
E-mail rockwines@lineone.net
Website www.pinotnoir.co.uk

Great Western Wine

Top-class Bath-based wine merchant.
The Wine Warehouse, Wells Road, Bath BA2 3AP
Tel 01225 322 800
Fax 01225 442 139
E-mail post@greatwesternwine.co.uk
Website www.greatwesternwine.co.uk

Handford

French fanciers in Holland Park, London.
12 Portland Road, London W11 4LE
Tel 020 7221 9614
Fax 020 7221 9613
E-mail james@handford-wine.demon.co.uk
Website www.handford-wine.demon.co.uk

Laithwaite's/Sunday Times Wine Club

Most successful mail-order merchants in UK with shop and e-commerce too.
New Acquitaine House, Exeter Way, Theale, Reading, Berkshire RG7 4PL
Tel 0870 444 8383
Fax 0870 444 8182
E-mail orders@laithwaites.co.uk
Website www.laithwaites.co.uk

Lay and Wheeler

Top notch all round.
Gosbecks Park, Gosbecks Road, Colchester, Essex CO2 9JT
Tel 0845 330 1855
Fax 01206 560 002
E-mail sales@laywheeler.com
Website www.laywheeler.com

Mayfair Cellars

Small London-based fine wine merchant.
203 Seagrove Road, Fulham, London SW6 1ST
Tel 020 7386 7999
Fax 020 7386 0202
E-mail esaunier@mayfaircellars.co.uk
Website www.mayfaircellars.co.uk

Portland Wine Company

Top class across-the-range rover.

16 North Parade, Sale, Manchester M33 3JS
Tel 0161 962 8752
Fax 0161 905 1291
E-mail portwineco@aol.com
Website www.portlandwine.co.uk

Raeburn Fine Wines

Thorough, well-maintained and exciting list.

21–23 Comely Bank Road, Edinburgh EH4 1DS
Tel 0131 343 1159
Fax 0131 332 5166
E-mail raeburnwines@btclick.com
Website www.raeburnfinewines.com

Turville Valley Wines

Sources the unsourceable, and the place to go for Domaine de la Romanée-Conti.

The Firs, Potter Row, Great Missenden, Buckinghamshire HP16 9LT
Tel 01494 868 818
Fax 01494 868 832
E-mail chris@turville-valley-wines.com
Website www.turville-valley-wines.com

T and W Wines

Where size matters: an enormous range.

51 King Street, Thetford, Norfolk IP24 2AU
Tel 01842 765 646
Fax 01842 766 407
E-mail contact@tw-wines.com
Website www.tw-wines.com

La Vigneronne

Feeling adventurous? Get on board this boat of unusual finds. Mainly French.

105 Brompton Road, London SW7 3LE
Tel 020 7589 6113
Fax 020 7581 2983
E-mail lavig@aol.com
Website www.lavigneronne.co.uk

Noel Young Wines

If you like Shiraz/Syrah, this is your man. With lots more besides.

56 High Street, Trumpington, Cambridge CB2 2LS
Tel 01223 844 744
Fax 01223 844 736
E-mail admin@nywines.co.uk
Website www.nywines.co.uk

How's your French?

Did you know that about 10 per cent of all wine consumed in England is bought in Calais? If you've got an articulated lorry to hand and a spare day to play with, then why not trot across to Calais and stock up for the season, saving up to 60 per cent on UK prices? If you're as greedy as me and as passionate about French food then you can gorge yourself over lunch in downtown Calais as well. Get your act together and there may be time for a walk along the beach or an invigorating paddle in the Channel.

Eating and Shopping in Calais

These are the best of a restaurant club with twelve member eateries (**www.toquesdopale.com**):

L'Aquar'Aile (great food, panoramic view over the sea)
Le Côte d'Argent (seafront, fantastic food)
La Pleiade (*astonishing* food)

I can also highly recommend:

Le Channel (phone number from here: 00 33 321 34 42 30): wonderful typical French food and jaw-dropping wine list.

Then if you've still got the energy to do a spot of shopping, take your pick from the following three main shopping areas:

The Centre Commercial Auchan Calais: Auchan hypermarket, Sainsbury's
Cité de l'Europe: Tesco, Oddbins, Carrefour
Zone Marcel Doret: Eastenders, Majestic, Pidoux, Perardel

To find out more go to **www.day-tripper.net**, an independent information site about booze day trips to Calais and other cross channel shopping.

CHAPTER SIX

Behind Bars

I AM VERY PLEASED TO SEE THAT THERE IS MORE WINE BEHIND bars these days. We have for too long been prisoners ourselves to a depressingly limited vinous choice in our drinking holes. Ten years ago in a traditional smog-filled, male drinking swamp (the great British pub) you'd have been lucky to find anything more appealing than a single optics rack with an upside-down two-litre bottle of warm Liebfraumilch, last replenished on the landlord's birthday. The City of London had housed old-school, dark-oak, dingy cellar drinking haunts for many many years, but these attracted grumpy, claret-drinking, fat-cigar smokers and were rarely frequented by women.

The 1970s brought a movement of basement 'wine bars' where the lone or group lesser-spotted female could be observed. These went out of fashion, though, about the same time as pop socks and pedal pushers, and unlike these fabulous fashion items have been slower to reinvent themselves. (The few that exist today are usually called the Grape Vine. They are stuck in a time warp, cluttered with wine paraphernalia, offering cold pork pies and still serving Mateus Rosé.) Wine served at theatre or cinema bars (if at all) would often have been better used for stripping set paint or removing the lead's stage make-up. All in all, it was a pretty dismal picture. Anyone of sound mind would be ashamed to be heard ordering a glass of wine in a pub. A lemonade shandy was, believe it or not, a less embarrassing alternative. It was as if the landlords themselves were chagrined about what they did (or didn't) have. Wine was hidden from view and stored incorrectly. Beer and spirits reigned supreme. You'd need a sniffer dog and a bottle detector to locate anything decent made from the grape.

By the 1990s, however, warning tremors of a 'wine in pubs revolution' were being felt around the country. As with all matters of a social concern, these started in culture-central London and other major cities. The scale of the task in hand made it clear that it would be a long journey to victory. By no means were we there yet. However, up sprung Pitcher and Pianos, All Bar Ones, Fine Lines and other wine-respecting establishments: female-friendly, bright and open drinking spaces, where wine was no longer the bar staff's humiliating secret but the focus of attention. Wine was on display in brightly labelled bottles. Actual 'pick up and hold' wine lists (i.e. a choice of more than two) were sitting waiting for you on the bar top or scrawled in chalk and begging to be read out from a blackboard above the barman's head.

What's more, many of these places were owned by breweries, who had surrendered to the fact that we, the customers, wanted wine – and if we didn't yet know we did, we would once we got it. New wines from the New World looked good on the bar, they discovered, offering flavours to tempt a new generation of largely female drinkers, with names they could confidently pronounce. Improving the wine offer was good for business. It attracted more women. Women, thanks to our pheromones and our handle on decision-making, would in turn provide more men.

Many of the big brewing boys have gone on to buy wine companies, realizing that this is now a way to bring in the bucks. Scottish and Newcastle, for example, have invested a vast amount to increase the presence of wine in their pubs and bars. They bought Waverley

Vintners and have together developed their own brand range from the New World. The Grape in Edinburgh is not coy about its vinous connection. The ceiling is covered in a fresco of all the world's winemaking regions and the back bar displays a range of thirty wines. The ultra-enthusiastic can do wine tastings there on a Tuesday evening as well: The Grape, 13 Capitol Building, St Andrews Square, Edinburgh, tel 0131 557 4522.

Young's pubs (of which there are well over two hundred round the country) began expanding their wine lists and now offer a phenomenal choice of wines by the glass, a move made to encourage the wine-shy out of their shells into tasting and enjoying wine, not just quaffing it. All this is helped by the introduction of wine-qualified bar staff (gasp!) – part of the emerging generation who know what it is they are serving us, even if we don't.

We have the established wine merchants of London to thank for breaking the dingy cellar 'wine bar' mould. Corney & Barrow and Lay & Wheeler have introduced a new wave of new-look wine bars to the City and beyond, with feature-length wine lists and much of the activity now taking place above ground. The look is glass-fronted, with ceiling spotlights, colourful fittings and squidgy leather sofas. They are pulling in a lunchtime crowd by offering trendy risotto-and-rocket-fuelled food, and a post-work, pinstripe mob, with incomes to dispose of, by offering Champagne and colourful cocktails. For more on these, visit Corney & Barrow at www.corney-barrow.co.uk, and Lay & Wheeler at www.lwwinebars.com.

Family-run merchants Davy's Wine Group and Balls Brothers have been offering their wine wares through drinking outlets in the City for far longer. Davy's have got into the swing of the 'chain' idea, bringing their twenty-plus wine bars into a twenty-first-century setting.

Balls Brothers have been slower to shake off their oak-panelled traditionalism, but newer additions to their collection are brighter, airier and increasingly focused on food. These are places where women can feel as comfortable as men. For more on these visit Davy's Wine Bars at www.davy.co.uk and Balls Brothers at www.ballsbrothers.co.uk.

As wine is not a natural part of our national heritage, it has taken us a long time to work out how well it goes with food. Food in pubs used to be employed as alcohol absorbent – it had no part to play in taste and pleasure. As it has improved, it has been greeted by an increasing choice of quality wines. The late-1990s advent of the good-grub gastropub has done wonders for improving and extending wine lists. Choosing wines that suit the style of food on offer is now a proprietor's prerogative (or should be). Selling wines by the glass gives the customer greater freedom to experiment and decide for herself.

Earthquake-scale ground was broken when London opened its first wine-themed attraction, Vinopolis, at the end of the 1990s. With it came the latest look in 'wine bar' design: the back to bricks and metal basics Wine Wharf. It has an amazing wine list you can taste through on a bar stool while watching the wall clocks showing the time in the wine regions of the world. Have a look at www.vinopolis.co.uk.

Getting served

Such is the progression of wine's status in today's drinking haunts that we are now faced with a new dilemma: having to select from a leviathan list of wines, many of whose names are unfamiliar, in a busy bar scrum on a Saturday night. Asking for any drink at all when engulfed in a ten-deep crush of bar queuers is a task for the toughest human being. Having to think about what you might want from a long list when put on the spot is close to impossible.

We have, on average, a total of about ten seconds in which to place our order at the bar. No wonder 'a glass of house wine, please' is so often requested under duress. Clever drinking holes have wine lists or cards on the tables around the room so that we can peruse the choice, consider what we feel like and practise pronunciation before heading into the heaving horde. If the list is written legibly on a blackboard then you should be able to see that from some distance (unless like me you are too vain to wear your glasses when you go out at night).

Many of the popular chain 'pubars', as I call them when they fall somewhere between a pub and a wine bar, make our decision even easier by stocking branded wines, whose names we are familiar with. The fridge at home is probably already full of Jacob's Creek and Blossom Hill, which begs us to ask the question why have we come out at all – to pay three or four times the price we did in the shop and get beaten about by a bunch of bar-barging bullies? Others compile a list of lesser-knowns or unknowns but try to include a few obvious or classic styles and a smattering of easily pronounceables. If they are generous, they might also include a brief description of what the wine should taste like. Retain a certain level of cynicism if every comment reads 'a delicious dry wine with lots of fruit and body'.

Knowing the style of wine you like can help if you get a chance to engage in actual conversation with the barperson rather than just miming 'a house', 'a glass' and 'a crushed grape'. You can ask them to choose for you, or to recommend a spicy, aromatic white or a light and fruity red, for example. Alternatively, if you don't see a particular wine on the list you know and like, you can always ask what they have got that's like Sancerre, or whatever.

Should you ask for a glass of dry wine and be served something that tastes like alcoholic grape juice with no milk and six sugars, you are perfectly entitled to return it and ask for something else. Wine in pubs and bars is expensive, sometimes the same price for a glass as it would be for a bottle of the same in a shop, so don't drink something you are not happy with.

The same rule applies in the nasty world of 'corked' wine. If you think there is something musty going on in your glass, don't be shy about saying so. It's not the landlord or bar manager's fault, remember, and they should, without querying it, open a new bottle and pour you a fresh glass. It's worth asking to try it this time. Give it a swirl, sniff, sip and then tip him/her a nod (and, if he's nice, a wink).

If you are ordering a bottle the barperson should automatically offer you a tasting sample. If you ask for a glass, you should be able to assume that the bartender has checked it beforehand. Often they do not, which is why shoddy goods slip through the net.

Of course, drinking out is not always a bun fight at the bar. There are many occasions when you can have a truly civilized experience, seated around a table or lounging on sofas, taking your time to think about what wines you'd like to try. Here's my plan to guide you through an evening of wine boozing with a gaggle of great mates.

The kick-off

The first drink is always the most exciting and often the most challenging to choose. What do I feel like? What am I in the mood for? Am I going to spoil myself? Can I think of a decent enough excuse to celebrate? A glass of bubbly has a feel-good factor about it that can't easily be beaten. It is best of all if you are out celebrating an achievement, good news or simply a reunion with old buddies, but it's perfectly acceptable if you just feel inclined to treat yourself. Champagne can, however, prove rather a costly rush of excitement, and you can often get as much of a thrill from a cheaper, sparkling wine alternative, something made by the same Traditional Method but from Australia, New Zealand or California. It should have more fruit and less acidity, as well, so might be easier on your empty stomach. Or for light-headed, gently spritzy fun, try Italy's Prosecco.

For the hard-headed who are used to spirits, I have two fortified-wine indiscretions to share, both of which are musts if the bar you are frequenting treats its customers to the odd olive or nutty nibble. Those of you who have been paying attention up till now will know what's coming. Fino sherry is a zesty, salty, tangy injection of flavour that electric-shocks your tastebuds into action for the night ahead and is so mouth-watering it ought to be served with a dribble-catching napkin. Portonic is the G'n'T or V'n'T addict's vinous alternative: a gorgeous, boozy, fruity aperitif made livelier still by a splash of cool tonic, ice and a slice. It's unforgivably good.

For the more cautious and calorie-conscious among you a spritzer is an easier-on-the-hips-and-head alternative to a straight glass of wine. Two-thirds of a glass of wine topped up with soda water allows you to comfortably consume the same amount of liquid but with less alcohol and fewer calories. Another keeping-it-together choice is German Riesling, a knee-weakening wine that has been horribly misconstrued. Not only is it light in alcohol (rarely more than 9 or 10 per cent), so you can drink a generous-sized glass of it, but it is also fragrantly perfumed, fabulously fruity and has a razor-sharp, refreshing burst of acidity to leave you drooling for days.

Getting stuck in

If you are out in a group, it's friendly and financially advisable to share a bottle of wine. If it's white you all agree on, then you need to gauge the way the group swings between dry and sweeter styles. Should you be divided, compromise by picking from somewhere in-between: ripe Australian Chardonnay can often have enough sweetness of fruit to keep those with sugar urges smiling. Or you can go for an off-dry to medium-sweet Vouvray or a German Kabinett or Spätlese wine.

Invigorating Whites

More often than not, we drink white wine because we are after something refreshing. Here is my list of wines that will hit the spots in need of invigoration.

* Pinot Grigio
* Muscadet
* Soave
* Albariño
* Unoaked Chardonnay (Chablis)
* Verdicchio
* Sancerre/Pouilly Fumé (Sauvignon Blanc)
* Alsace whites
* Gavi di Gavi

Embracing Whites

If, on the other hand, it's miserable outside and you are feel a bit self-sorry, you will want to snuggle down in the sofa with a glass of heart-warming comfort. Here's my list of richer whites which, although still served chilled, will reach out and hug you tightly in a giant flavour-filled embrace.

* White burgundy or any other oaked Chardonnay from anywhere in the world
* Oaky Semillon

* Oaky Verdelho
* White Rioja
* Fumé Blanc (oaked Sauvignon Blanc)
* Rhône white or any Viognier, Marsanne or Roussanne
* Oaked Chenin Blanc

Rosés

When the jury is hung between red and white then rosé is the obvious concession. There may not be a huge choice in a rural British drinking hole or a busy city bar, however. Rosés are most at home on the beach, after all. But if you can find one from Bandol (southern French), Tavel (Rhône), South America or Spain, then you should be in line for something characterful and fruity. It may be a single varietal rosé, in which case it should say Syrah or Cabernet Sauvignon or so on on the label. Otherwise it will be a mix of various suitables commonly known as a blend.

Light Reds

If you are a white wine lover being press-ganged by your fellow drinkers into choosing red, then suggest one of the following, which are light in tannins and should be easy on the teeth and gums.

* Beaujolais or Gamay from anywhere
* Rioja or another Tempranillo
* An older Chianti
* Pinot Noir
* Barbera or Dolcetto from Italy or anywhere

Big Reds

If you are in the mood for a serious and contemplative red to mull over as you consider world domination or at least debate British politics, then here is my list of big reds to get your gums around. But watch out with these blockbusters. They may make you supremely confident of your position in an argument over the future of the NHS, for example, but they might not do your own personal health the best possible service. Most of these reds will have a minimum of 13.5 per cent alcohol, some of them as much as 14.9 per cent (and 15 per cent is the legal minimum for *fortified* wine).

* Californian Zinfandel
* Rhône reds or any Syrah (Shiraz) or Grenache
* Bordeaux, or Cabernet Sauvignon, Merlot, Cabernet Franc from anywhere
* Barolo or Barbaresco from Italy or Nebbiolo from anywhere
* Negroamaro
* Southern French reds
* Pinotage from South Africa
* Portuguese reds
* Carmenère

Winding down

Winding down an evening is as important as making sure it kicks off with a bang (or other appropriate explosive cork noise). A vinous nightcap is a fitting conclusion. Something sweet and sinful works best for me every time. Port, sweet oak-matured sherry or Madeira are all decadent mouthfuls of dried fruit, treacle, spice and all the other puddingy flavours of Christmas – only they don't have to be relegated to then. Sip on one of these as you contemplate the best mode of transport home (which does not, of course, include driving).

A word in your ear

At this point, I must point out that my lists are not intended to encourage you to exceed the recommended sensible drinking limit of three units of wine a day (see page 244 for more on sensible limits). That's three standard-sized glasses of any of my suggestions.

One final word of warning, ladies, as you busily powder your nose in preparation for your night out on the vine. Make sure you order enough water to have a constant supply with you throughout the evening. Still is better than fizzy, because fizzy contains more sodium (salt), which makes you thirstier and also makes you burp. Don't let the devil dehydration ruin your fun with wine.

CHAPTER SEVEN

In Restaurants

THERE'S A MAN WEARING SMART TROUSERS AND A WAISTCOAT standing over me. He has a white napkin resting over his forearm, and he's looking at me with a puzzled, slightly shocked expression on his face. I am feeling acutely self-conscious. I am wondering if my shirt buttons have come undone or if I have insulted his family. But then I remember. I simply asked if I could see the wine list. Even in this time of equal pay opportunities, chairwomen and husbands who stay at home ironing blouses, women are not supposed to ask for the wine list in a restaurant, order a bottle of wine or sample it to see if it's acceptable to drink. That, my friends, is still a man's job.

I had to go to the extreme length of writing this book in order to gain the credibility to be given the wine list to look at. And even so, the men I eat with have to explain to the wine waiter, 'Don't worry, it's all right, she works in wine, she knows what she's doing.' (For the sake of simplicity in this chapter I am making the wine waiter a man. It saves all that 'he or she' business. There are an increasing number of wine waitresses out there, but it has to be said that they get trained to approach the male diner first too.) The only other way to be in with a real chance of landing the role of wine chooser is to only ever eat out with women.

The sad result of this prejudice is that many of us

women believe we don't know how to order wine in a restaurant. The truth is that even men find wine lists confusing. Most of them are just too proud to admit it, or too worried that we'll think less of them if they do. And wine lists can be brain-teasingly complex, not to mention long.

The first rule is not to be ashamed of admitting you're not sure what to choose. You wouldn't feel embarrassed to ask what the soup of the day was or whether there were peanuts in the stir-fry, so why not ask which wine would be best with your Caesar salad or what the Chilean Carmenère will taste like? If nothing else, engaging in conversation and building a good relationship with your wine waiter (and flirting with him outrageously if this is necessary/desirable) is likely to get you better service overall. Besides which, it can be very satisfying for him to show off his vinous knowledge to a receptive customer. (Assuming he *has* vinous knowledge. The alternative is not worth contemplating.)

Trust the waiter. It would be very hard for a waiter to rip you off and anyway he doesn't want to. The only time you might need to be on the ball is if the waiter recommends something not on the list, or, worse still, the restaurant is so posh they don't publish prices. Then ask how much the wine costs because it might be something that would alarm even the best-prepared wallet.

The wine list

You might be given a small piece of card, or an inch-thick encyclopedia. The wine on the list could be set out in any of a number of ways. Most lists have a 'house wine' section, otherwise referred to as 'sommelier recommendations' or 'cellar selection'. The rest of the collection might be divided up by country, grape variety or, more fashionable recently, style. Some are listed in ascending price order within their groupings, and others are all jumbled up. Mixing them up is a nifty ploy to deter you from leaping on the first wine on the list, encouraging you therefore to take a deeper, braver (and possibly more expensive) look.

If the list is divided up by country, don't be surprised to see that France typically hogs more space than any other country (apart from the obvious exceptions, where you are eating Italian or the proprietor is a self-confessed Australophile, for example). The UK imports a vast amount of wine from France, and why not? It hasn't got far to travel, it's notoriously well-matched with food and the range of styles and flavours are almost unrivalled elsewhere. Also, for people interested in spending big money on complex, mature wines from renowned vintages, either to impress clients or simply spoil themselves, then Bordeaux, Burgundy and the Rhône (all French regions) are where the serious contenders can be found. And France is the home of the world's finest sparkling wine as well: Champagne.

France is, of course, not without competition, and these days restaurateurs have widened the range on their radars and are increasing the international choice on their wine lists. Wines that were once fashionable are making a flares-style comeback – German and Portuguese, for example – while other, newer entries are soaring up the charts: Australia, New Zealand, South America and South Africa, in particular.

Restaurant-food-friendly grape varieties are increasingly being added to up-to-the-minute restaurants' lists as well. In the white camp are characters such as Riesling, Pinot Gris/Grigio, Arneis, Viognier and Albariño, and in the red zone are Merlot, Malbec and Pinot Noir, as well as natives from Portugal and southern Italy.

Introducing the food-friendly grapes

Riesling, the classic grape of Germany and Alsace, has had a tough time making friends ever since it was wrongly associated with Liebfraumilch, the sad sugar-water export of Germany. What more and more restaurateurs (though, sadly, not enough yet) are realizing is that it is one of the world's most interesting varieties, with a rarely rivalled capacity to age and fantastic compatibility with oriental cuisine and all the flavours of the east. Its naturally aromatic, floral fragrance, sometimes slightly sweet palate and steely acidity make it an instinctive bed partner for spicy, strongly scented food. Try Riesling with a Chinese stir-fry or Thai curry and prepare to be amazed. Australian and New Zealand examples are richer and fruitier in flavour still and must also be part of your next experimental experience.

Radical Riesling supporters include the Cherwell Boathouse in Oxford, whose list features examples from all corners of the wine globe (tel 01865 552 746; website www.cherwellboathouse.co.uk). The restaurant is a converted boathouse on the banks of the Cherwell river and the food is top notch as well. They fully encourage their women customers to order and taste first, instead of the men. And Newport House, Newport, in County Mayo, Ireland, is another place for Riesling, and you can also find Claret back to 1961 as a bonus (tel +353 098 41222; website www.newporthouse.ie).

Pinot Grigio is the cheap, bland staple of most Italian restaurants, but have you tried Pinot Gris, its alter ego from Alsace, Oregon or New Zealand? It's the same but very different indeed, offering some of the aromatic character of Riesling but with a broad, round, comforting palate similar to that of Chardonnay as well. Excellent with new-wave cooking, spicy flavours and rich sauces. Another Riesling look-alike, food-friendly must-try is Italian Arneis from Roero in the northern region of Piemonte, again for spicy, eastern food and seafood.

Viognier, now from all over the globe (though originating in Condrieu in France's Rhône valley), was at one point heralded as the new Chardonnay. It is at least proving itself a competent contender for strong, rich, spicy foods. Its apricot and spice intensity is making its mark in restaurants across the country, though I do think that some of the sweeter, high-alcohol versions can be too much.

If fish is your dish then the latest vinous Match of the Day is Albariño, a peachy, fresh, floral, slightly spicy, super-refreshing variety from the rain-soaked northern Spanish region of Galicia.

Merlot, in addition to its legendary guise as the more significant part of the magical combination that makes up the reds of St Emilion and Pomerol of Bordeaux, is a must-stock on any wine list these days. Examples from Chile, New Zealand and Australia are full of food-friendly flavours: easy to drink, and providing a bill at the end that is easy to swallow. Malbec is the other South American success story to hit our wine-list headlines. Dark and plummy, it's a red-meat match every time.

Pinot Noir doesn't have to come from Burgundy. It is often more affordable if you pick it out from somewhere else, such as the United States, New Zealand, Tasmania, Victoria in Australia or Walker Bay in South Africa. A lighter-style red, it is soft and raspberry-ish when young (as it is most often found from these New World regions) and, surprising for a red, even do-able with fish.

The Portuguese are given praise for their port and even occasionally for their Madeira but rarely for their table wines. Until recently, that is. Now they have started offering rich juicy reds at cash-comfy prices, needy of flavour-rich, spicy foods. Look out for them coming on to restaurant lists.

Finally, southern Italy and Sicily are the homes of soft ripe reds perfect for pasta'n'pizza but just as worthy of an intensely flavoured stew. Look out for names such as Salice Salentino, Aglianico del Vulture, Taurasi and Nero d'Avola.

If you haven't tried any of the above then do yourself a flavour favour next time you are eating out and give them a go. If you are desperately seeking to break from the norm but still don't know which way to turn, try to find a restaurant like White Moss House at Grasmere in the Lake District (tel 01539 435 295; website www.whitemoss.com), where they help you sniff out New World equivalents to the famous European classics by listing them at the end of each European section. You can also try classic old vintages here at reasonable mark-ups.

There are still too many eating establishments reluctant either to experiment themselves or to encourage their customers to do so, who stick with the predictable branded classics of Chablis, Chianti, Rioja, Sancerre, Côtes-du Rhône and don't try to offer alternatives that might make an even more memorably mouth-watering match than these stalwart usuals. Businesses won't risk filling their cellars with unusual wines they might not shift – especially so long as we customers always give in to the reassuring tug of the familiar.

House wines and wine by the glass

For many years we've been held hostage by house wines. Only one choice, red or white, the cheapest wine the proprietor could find that wouldn't actually burn your lips. Faced with that, or wading through a bible-sized wine list with nothing but unpronounceable names in every language but your mother tongue, how much easier was it to ask for the house wine? Two simple words that you could only mess up if it was your fourth bottle and you were dining alone. Unequivocally it is the easiest option, and happily in most places now it isn't always bad. If only the alternative was made more accessible to us, both mentally and financially. Then perhaps we wouldn't display such reluctance to forsake the reassurance of the house wine.

An increasing number of hotels, restaurants and gastro-pubs are, however, beginning to give us a chance to experiment – with new-found confidence and without remortgaging the house – by offering a range of house wines instead of just one or two. Up to twenty or thirty in some places, though usually about ten, these wines are in effect the restaurant or sommelier's specific recommendations, offering affordability and quality. The restaurant chose these for a specific reason and so should, in theory, know them well and be able to guide you through them. What's more, the customer – and this is where the fun starts – is required to take the plunge by saying something other than 'the house wine, please'.

Another safety net that various restaurants are now stringing up is wine by the glass or in half-bottles. This way you can try wines you would ordinarily pass straight over, and even if you're not convinced when you get to the end of it, the worst you've done is 37.5cl of damage, and the best is only 25cl.

The best bit of buying by the glass is that you can venture into the much-maligned and apparently law-bound world of food and wine matching by trying different wines with each of your courses. You could easily notch up four different wines over a three-course meal: an aperitif, one with your starter, one with your main course and something sweet and sinful with your pudding or cheese.

One of the extremist wine-by-the-glass restaurants is the charming Crooked Billet country pub in Newton Longville, Buckinghamshire (tel 01908 373 936; website www.thebillet.co.uk), where over two hundred and seventy wines by glass should satisfy even the most far-reaching wine explorer. So too should the three hundred possibilities at Brown's Hotel Restaurant 1837 on

Albemarle Street, Mayfair, London (tel 020 7493 6020, website www.brownshotel.com): you'll have to reach deep into your pockets if you go there. Plenty of by-the-glass enthusiasm can be found at the Fat Duck in Bray, Berkshire, where everything bar the oldest and rarest can be enjoyed that way (tel 01628 580 333; website www.fatduck.co.uk).

With a growing number of food-friendly varieties appearing on lists, and the arrival of new styles from the New World and even some changing styles from the Old, it seems a shame not to try to find the most harmonious combination of vine and victuals you can. Restaurants who'd like to aid you in finding the perfect partnering include the Sharrow Bay Hotel with its breathtaking view over Ullswater in Cumbria (tel 01768 486 301; website www.sharrow-bay.com), the Pheasant at Ross-on-Wye in Herefordshire (tel 01989 565 751) and Adlard's in Upper St Giles Street, Norwich (tel 01603 633 522; website www.adlards.co.uk).

The sport of matching wine to food has as many detractors as fans. Some think it's restrictive and even passé. Have you ever thought of reversing the trend? Why not be utterly original and choose the wine first and let the food follow?

By the glass: aperitif

To whet your appetite while you pore over the tummy-tormenting menu, you'll need an aperitif – by the glass, of course. Champagne or sparkling wine is a predictable but reliable option, one whose tongue-teasing acidity never fails to get the gastric juices looking lively. Of course, *the* drink to be seen about town with is Portonic. Served on the rocks with a slice of lemon, it's fruity and refreshing and works for me every time. Or try a *copita* of Spanish Fino or Manzanilla sherry (*not* Harvey's Bristol Cream). These are zingy, citric, nutty meal-starters. Regrettably, restaurants are not always the best places for sherry.

A fresh, young style such as Fino or Manzanilla must be drunk icy chilled from a bottle opened no more than two or three days before. A few great restaurants where the owners are defenders of the sherry faith are: Gaudi, the modern Spanish set-up on Clerkenwell Road in London (tel 020 7608 3220; website www.turnmills.co.uk), Lomo, my favourite tapas joint on the Fulham Road in London (tel 020 7349 8848; website www.lomo.co.uk), and La Trompette, fancy French food on Devonshire Road, London (tel 020 8747 1836). Find out more at www.london-eating.co.uk/1638.htm. Outside of London, try the traditional St Tudno Hotel in Llandudno, Wales (tel 01492 874 411; website www.st-tudno.co.uk). All part of the Huntsbridge group and sharing the same extensive wine list are the Three Horseshoes thatched inn in Madingley, Cambridgeshire (tel 01954 210 221; look up www.beerguide.co.uk/towns/madingley.htm), the Falcon at Fotheringhay, Northants (tel 01832 226 254), the Old Bridge Hotel in Huntingdon, Cambridgeshire (tel 01480 424 300) and the Pheasant at Keyston, Cambridgeshire (tel 01832 710 241).

Ordering your wine

So you've made your choice. If pronouncing funny foreign words makes you trip over your tongue and blush like a naughty schoolgirl, you may prefer to ask for the wine by number or by pointing it out on the list, but I recommend you give the pronunciation of the name a go. If the waiter's multilingual and you've got it wrong, he can correct you and you'll come away from the meal knowing more than you did when you went there. If he's not, he won't know you've got it wrong anyway. If it's just you and a man you are desperately keen to impress and you think you might blow it, go armed with a snazzy napkin trick to wow him with afterwards. (Anyway, I'd like to hear him do better.)

If you are ordering a bottle of red wine that's over five years old (look at the vintage), your waiter should ask if you want it decanted (for more on decanting see page 99). If you're not sure, take his advice on this. Alternatively, take the bottle in your own hands, hold it up to the light and look for obvious sediment at the bottom. The most important reds to decant are Bordeaux (or equivalent blend from somewhere like Western Australia, California or South Africa), most serious Cabernet Sauvignons, Rhônes, some big Australian Shirazes and, of course, Vintage or Crusted port.

Decanting is generally reserved for smarter establishments who stock old and wise, deep-pocket-searching wines from legendary vintages. At the extreme opposite end, in cheap European bistros you may well find a jug of wine is plonked on the table, siphoned on many occasions straight from a tank or barrel out back.

You should expect red wine to be offered to you at room temperature (unless it's a Beaujolais or other light low-tannin red) – put your hands round the bottle and you will be able to tell quite easily if it is. If you ordered white or fizzy it should be offered to you between 6 and 13°C, depending on its style, but basically well chilled.

The waiter should show you the label to allow you to check that this bottle is what you've asked for. If you confirm it is, he should open it. He may go on to sniff the cork, then offer it to you to see if you want to examine it. This largely outmoded tradition dates back to the eighteenth century when showing you the cork proved that the restaurant wasn't ripping you off by refilling great wine bottles with plonk. Not something we have to worry much about these days. The sniffing of the cork is also rather a wasted exercise because it's often impossible to tell in this way if a wine is corked (tainted by a musty-smelling mould that grows in over 1 per cent of corks). To do this you need to sniff the wine in the glass.

Now the waiter pours you a small tasting sample. Give the glass a good swirl and then take a long, hard sniff. Does it smell fresh, fruity and inviting or like a mouldy old mushroom dug up from a damp cellar? If it's the latter, the wine is corked, and you are well within your rights to inform the waiter and ask for another bottle. In fact, you'd be mad not to. It's not the restaurant's fault; they didn't know it was corked until they opened it for you. Otherwise, if the wine doesn't smell right or look the colour you were expecting, it could be oxidized or volatile (see pages 52–3). It's worth confirming your initial nasal assessment by taking a sip. Some faults are more easily detected by tasting, and you might prefer a wine's flavour to its smell.

In wine there is often more scope for personal taste than in food. It is only acceptable to send food back if there is something wrong with it, if it is mouldy, smells bad or contains a foreign body. But if you don't like a wine, for whatever reason, few restaurants will refuse to swap your choice for something else. The key is to display resounding confidence in your view while trying not to sound uppity, rude or ready to step outside for a fight.

If the wine smells and tastes good, tip the waiter a nod or a wink and he can continue pouring – the others at the table first, then returning to you. The glass should only ever be filled half full so that you can swirl it and liberate the wine's aroma and flavours. Once he's done the rounds and if there's some wine left in the bottle of white, then he can put it into the ice bucket, which should contain a mixture of water and ice, preferably with a napkin over the top of it so that you can wipe the bottom dry when you come to repour. If there is any red left in the bottle, that can go straight down on the table.

What's left to do but keep the wine flowing? If you finish a bottle of wine and ask for another one, the same procedure of having a sample first should apply. Watch out for waiters who begin pouring into the first empty glass they spy on the table. They might get halfway round before anybody notices it's corked.

When ordering wine by the glass, it's unlikely you'll be shown the bottle. Just remember the guidelines for temperature are the same, as are what to do if it's corked or you simply don't like it.

What if you hit it off so well with a wine you want to invite it into your house for a more intimate encounter at a later date? That's fine if you can find it in the shops, but not all wines on restaurant lists are readily available in retail outlets. Some restaurateurs actively avoid serving wines you'll recognize from the shops so you can't see how much more they are charging than the retail price (their 'mark-up'). Restaurants with wine shops attached are the obvious answer to your prayers; otherwise ask the restaurant owner where he gets the wine from and see if his supplier will sell you a case direct. If this and all else fails, you can always find the same style of wine from a different producer and take your experiment a step further.

Alternatively, you might want to take home at the end of the evening a bottle that you haven't quite managed to empty. If you've come to the end of the meal or are committed to the steering wheel of your car, you might want to save your new-found vinous friend for finishing off before bed. Some restaurants will allow you to do this. If you are lucky enough to live near the Pheasant at Ross-on-Wye in Herefordshire, for example, you can take advantage of their great country-style cooking, their 'try before you buy' wine policy, their easy-to-use 'search by style, variety or food match' wine list, and still recork and take home your half-finished bottle at the end of the night. These guys want to make life easy and fun for you (tel 01989 565 751).

By the glass: finishing off

Spoil yourself at the end of the meal as you have done at the beginning. Undo the top button on your skirt to make room for the long-lusted-after dessert and order yourself a sweet wine by the glass to go with it. A multitude of different styles of dessert wine, ranging from light, fruity and honeyed (an Auslese Riesling from Germany, for example) to dark brown, dried fruit and treacle types (such as a Liqueur Muscat from Australia), exist to offer extremes of oral pleasure. The key when making your choice is to try to find one sweeter than your pudding, otherwise the pudding runs the risk of making the wine taste slightly bland and dull: a waste of one of life's greatest indulgences, I reckon.

The dessert-wine dedicated (other than the author of this book) can be found at Noble Rot on Mill Street in London's West End (tel 020 7629 8877; website www.noblerot.com), named after the harmless mould (*Botrytis cinerea*) that shrivels up and concentrates the sugars in the great grapes of Sauternes from France and Tokaji from Hungary. Also try the Harrow Inn in Little Bedwyn, Wiltshire, where their Canadian Ice Wine is a must-try for those on a big budget (tel 01672 870 871; website www.harrowinn.co.uk). In the Three Horseshoes in Madingley, Cambridgeshire, they are as excited about dessert wines as they are about sherry; try them or any of the others in the Huntsbridge group (see above).

The mark-up

So you've ordered, sampled and drunk your fill and are feeling fantastically empowered for doing it, if not a little light-headed as well. Now comes the unfun part – the bill. Make sure you are sitting down when it arrives. Wine mark-ups in restaurants can be eye-wateringly high – often as much as 300 or 400 per cent. Surprising, you might think, when all the restaurant is doing is storing it and taking the cork out.

In certain restaurants the wine bottle does get more tender loving care than in others. Expensive older wines may have been cellared for a long time and need gentle handling during decanting. But, perhaps more to the point, we are generally less questioning about paying a lot for wine (especially if we don't know its real value) than paying a lot for food. So wine is where the restaurateur can make a profit. If there is money to be made from mark-ups then you can bet your life most restaurateurs will do it to cover overheads and staff. We probably have to accept that sky-high prices are what you pay in order to take part in the whole dining-out experience, but I have no doubt that people would buy more and better wine if the mark-ups were not so alarming. This would in turn increase their overall interest in wine and, in the long run, feed more money back into the restaurants. Until that happens, I shall sing the praises of BYO.

The benefits of BYO

The law in the UK is pretty flexible about whether you buy in-house or Bring Your Own, so it's down to the individual establishment. Restaurants that offer BYO take fewer money risks by not investing in and storing wine that might not shift. For the customer, it's the perfect way to keep the bank manager off your back (as long as the corkage charge is not taking the mickey), while enjoying wines you already know or trying new ones out with previously untasted dishes.

Sadly there are not nearly enough unlicensed eating outlets in the UK. BYO is much more popular in major-wine producing countries. Australians, for example, go raving mad for it, especially in restaurants established near to wineries. A community conscience in wine areas means it's in everyone's interests to encourage the sharing of wines and even ideas. Paradoxically, however, many restaurants in wine-producing areas are not able to offer the range that we, one of the most zealous wine-importing countries in the world, can offer to thirsty visitors.

Here is my pick of BYOs, worth seeking out if you are in the area. They tend to be low-maintenance eateries with cheap 'n' cheerful food – places to go when you have just had an unhappy chat with Mr Bank.

Corkage is the fee that most places charge for letting you bring your own wine and lending you their corkscrew. They will probably even open the bottle for you and also refrigerate your whites. It's best to ring and check in advance if you are planning to take a truckload.

Beanscene

Tapas and fusion fun. Corkage: £2 a bottle (after 6 p.m.).
Decourcy's Arcade, 5–21 Cresswell Lane, Glasgow G12
Tel 0141 334 6776

Blah Blah Blah

A top vegetarian place where the food is so full of flavour and texture you can easily be fooled into thinking you are eating meat – if that's what you like. Corkage: £1.25 per head (not per bottle).
78 Goldhawk Road, London W12 8HA
Tel 020 8746 1337

Books for Cooks

A fun café in a bookshop with a different recipe from one of the books to try each day. Corkage: none. Corney and Barrow very handily next door.
4 Blenheim Crescent, London W11 1NN
Tel 020 7221 1992

The Egg Café

Vegetarian and vegan food. Corkage: £1 a bottle.
16-21 Newington Buildings, Liverpool L1 4ED
Tel 0151 707 2755

Jigglers Restaurant

Global food. Corkage: £1 per bottle.
62 Andersontown Road, Belfast BT11 9AN
Tel 02890 285 454

Lemongrass

Thai cuisine. Corkage: £2.50 per head (to encourage people to bring as much as they like, and if they can't finish it the staff are willing to help).

19 Copson Street, Withington, Manchester M20 3HE
Tel 0161 434 2345

Rogan's Vegetarian

As it says. Corkage: none.

12 College Road, Handsworth Road, Birmingham B20 2HX
Tel 0121 515 3906

Thai Corner Café

Fabulous Thai food. Corkage: £1.50 a bottle.

44 North Cross Road, Dulwich, London SE22 9EU
Tel 020 8299 4041

The middle ground of course is to BYO to a licensed restaurant. Funnily enough it tends only to be people in the wine trade who have the cheek to do this, although there is no reason why anyone shouldn't. After all, the worst the owner can say is no. Many top restaurants will agree to it as long as you buy something from their list as well. They also prefer it if you discuss it with them when you make the booking and pay a nominal corkage fee of on average about £10 a bottle. Some won't charge you anything, but this is the exception rather than the rule.

Any serious wine from older vintages is far more cheaply consumed this way. And if you also have to choose something from their list, you get the added benefits of trying wines you might not find anywhere else or that might be particularly suited to their menu.

In the same vein as Happy Hour, some licensed restaurants offer BYO on certain nights of the week. Here are a few I know of:

Scoffers

6 Battersea Rise, London, SW11 1ED
Tel 020 7978 5542 – on Mondays

Bathtub Bistro

2 Grove Street, Bath BA2 6PJ
Tel 01225 460 593 and
No. 5 Bistro, 5 Argyle Street, Bath BA2 4BA
Tel 01225 444 499 – on Mondays and Thursdays

Gingerhill

1 Hillhead Street, Milngavie, Glasgow G62 8AF
Tel 0141 956 6515 – Thursday to Saturday nights

The final trick is to hunt out cafés or restaurants that own wine shops as well. If the shop is attached then you only have to pop next door, returning armed and ready. The Wine Gallery in Hollywood Road, West London (tel 020 7352 7572) has a shop next door. The prices in the restaurant and the shop are the same. If something is not in stock in the restaurant they will fetch it from the shop for you.

In Valvona and Crolla Caffè Bar, 19 Elm Row, Edinburgh EH7 4AA (tel 0131 556 6066; website www.valvonacrolla.com), you can buy wine from the attached wine shop, which specializes in Italian wines, and pay £4 corkage before 6 p.m. and £8 thereafter to drink them in the café. A serious selection to choose from.

More Choices

Other restaurants not mentioned above and what makes their wine lists worth stopping at nothing to get at.

Angel Inn

By glass, great value.
Hetton, North Yorkshire BD23 6LT
Tel 01756 730 263
Website www.angelhetton.co.uk

Bleeding Heart

For Francophiles. Happy for you to BYO at £10 corkage per bottle.
Bleeding Heart Yard, Greville Street, London EC1N 8SJ
Tel 020 7242 8238.
Website www.bleedingheart.co.uk

Cambio de Tercio

Spanish admirers.

163 Brompton Road, London SW5 OLJ

Tel 020 7244 8970

With a tapas bar at 174 Brompton Road where they allow BYO at £2 corkage per bottle.

Tel 020 7370 3685

Cayenne

Wines listed by grape variety.

7 Ascot House, Shaftesbury Square, Belfast BT2 7DB

Tel 02890 331 532

Website www.cayennerestaurant.com

Cellar

Germany and Alsace.

24 East Green, Anstruther, Fife, Scotland, KY10 3AA

Tel 01333 310 378

Croque en Bouche

Lengthy wine list can be downloaded from the website in advance or if it's too much on the day choose from shorter 'wines by style' list.

221 Wells Road, Malvern Wells, Worcestershire WR14 4HF

Tel 01684 565 612

Website www.croque-en-bouche.co.uk

The Cross

Refreshingly original – no house wines and no French. The wine list is talked through by the enthusiastic owner.

The Old Tweed Mill, Ardbroilach Road, Kingussie, Inverness-shire, Scotland PH21 1LB

Tel 01540 661 166

Website www.thecross.co.uk

Gidleigh Park

Mark-ups fair considering the quality of this outstanding list.

Chagford, Devon TQ13 8HH

Tel 01647 432 367

Website www.gidleigh.com

Hotel du Vin

What you might expect from the name. Five hotels with restaurants in Birmingham, Winchester, Tunbridge Wells, Bristol and Brighton. Sources of rare, traditional and innovative choices.

Head office 12 Southgate Street, Winchester S023 9EF

Tel 01962 850 676

Website www.hotelduvin.com

Inverlochy Castle

Pages and pages of half-bottles.

Torlundy, Fort William, Scotland PH33 6SN

Tel 01397 702 177

Website www.inverlochycastlehotel.co.uk

Michael's Nook Country House Hotel

Lesser-known regions, value pricing, top food.

Grasmere, Cumbria LA22 9RP

Tel 01539 435 496

Website www.grasmere-hotels.co.uk

Sir Charles Napier

Informative list to help you decide.

Spriggs Alley, Chinnor, Oxfordshire OX9 4BX

Tel 01494 483 011

Odette's

Plenty of choice on the wine list under £25. Modern British cuisine with a wine bar downstairs serving brasserie-style food.

130 Regent's Park Road, London NW1 8XL

Tel 020 7586 5486

The Pelican

Certified organic gastro-pub. Wines only from Europe but all from small independent organic and biodynamic producers.

45 All Saints Road, Ladbroke Grove, London W11 1HE

Tel 020 7792 3073

Website www.singhboulton.co.uk/pelican.html

They also have the Crown at Victoria Park and the Duke in Islington; see website for details.

Porthole Eating House

German supporters.

3 Ash Street, Bowness-on Windermere, Cumbria LA23 3EB

Tel 01529 442 793

Website www.porthole.fsworld.co.uk

Le Poussin at Parkhill

Thirty wines by the glass and half-bottles.

Beaulieu Road, Lyndhurst, Hampshire S043 7FZ

Tel 02380 282 944

Website www.lepoussin.co.uk

Ransome's Dock

Modern European cuisine – digestif and dessert experts.

35–37 Parkgate Road, London SW11 4NP

Tel 020 7223 1611

Website www.ransomesdock.co.uk

RSJ

Loire wines of every style.
13A Coin Street, London SE1 8YQ
Tel 020 7928 4554
Website www.rsj.uk.com

Sheen Falls Lodge, La Cascade

950 wines on list, with maps of major wine regions to put it all in context.
Kenmare, Co Kerry, Republic of Ireland
Tel +353 064 41600
Website www.sheenfallslodge.ie

Square

Rare vintage Champagnes and French wines.
6–10 Bruton Street, London W1X 7AG
Tel 020 7495 7100

Summer Isles Hotel

Over 50 half-bottles.
Achiltibuie, Ross-shire, Scotland IV26 2YG
Tel 01854 622 282
Website www.summerisleshotel.co.uk

Le Talbooth

South Africa.
Gun Hill, Dedham, Colchester CO7 6HP
Tel 01206 323 150
Website www.talbooth.com

Terre à Terre

All organic and vegetarian wines; global vegetarian food.
71 East Street, Brighton BN1 1HQ
Tel 01273 729 051

Vineyard at Stockcross

California crazy.
Stockcross, Berkshire RG20 8JU
Tel 01635 528 770
Website www.the-vineyard.co.uk

Zafferano

Italiano.
15 Lowndnes Street, London SW1X 9EY
Tel 0207 235 5800

CHAPTER EIGHT

Accessorizing

IS IT JUST THE WOMEN IN *MY* FAMILY OR ARE ALL WOMEN nominated present-buyers from birth? My dad, brother and other half were clearly assigned the role of last-minute card co-signer when God was casting life parts for everyone. If you are always the one left to hunt for the ultimate wedding, christening, bar mitzvah or birthday present and are running out of fresh ideas, here is a list of gifts that are related in some way to wine, plus why anyone might want or need them and how they actually work. I've also suggested who they might be most appropriate for, from your bibulous boss to your sherry-sipping grandma.

The gift victim (or recipient, as they are more commonly termed) might possibly not have a specific enthusiasm for wine, but there will doubtless be the odd suitable occasion when their fashionable wine accessory will smarten up a dinner party or at least give observant guests something to talk about. Wine itself even makes a good christening present. The little noise-maker may be too young to fully appreciate it at first, but your gift of age-able wine will increase in value and complexity over time – and you can't say that about computers, bicycles or mobile phones. Antique wine gifts might be appreciated more by age-advanced friends and relatives. My suggestion is to pick something you like yourself and if you're very lucky they might leave it to you in their will.

Remember that a wine accessory is also a solution to that dreaded conundrum of what to give the man who has everything. He cannot possibly have 'everything' listed below. Some of these are for aesthetic pleasure, and some are techno-gadgety. I'm left wondering what there remains to invent. If I could think of it, I'd be on to it in a flash.

Decanters and Associated Paraphernalia

Decanters come in many shapes and sizes, most of them graceful. Many are made of crystal with bulbous bottoms and narrow necks and a stopper to keep the wine from going off (oxidizing) too quickly. Mind you, you can decant wine into almost anything you like. Sometimes a small rustic jug is more appropriate for your red wine and just as pretty on a lunch table. The more interesting decanters are the 'pass the port', 'hoggit' and 'turn' decanters, which have a pointed bottom so that you can't hoggit (put it down beside you) but instead have to keep it on the move, returning it to the wooden base traditionally held on to by the host or the head of the family. Based on a different principle is the broad-bottomed ship's decanter whose wide flat base keeps it steady at sea. You can decant white wine as well. Most white wine decanters are taller, thinner and more tapered than red wine decanters because they don't need the same breadth for airing, swilling and swirling.

Decanter Dryers

A vessel with a narrow neck is virtually impossible to dry on the inside. Thus the invention of the decanter dryer, elegant, typically wooden racks that hold the decanter upside-down to dry. Most are made for two. For anyone with a decanter already or, if you are feeling super generous, to give alongside a decanter as a wedding present or a house-warming gift for someone close to you, a family member or best friend.

Decanting Machines

You need a steady hand for decanting very old, heavily sedimented wines, or you could use a decanting machine. This clever device holds the wine bottle tightly in a horizontal pouring position. You wind the handle and pour the wine into the decanter over the light from a torch or flame. (See Chapter Four for a decanting lesson.) This is for someone who takes decanting seriously and has a collection of very old bottles they want to show off. A great anniversary present for an elderly couple whose pouring technique might be a bit shaky.

Decanting Funnels

A funnel takes away the risk of you slopping half your family's fortune of wine straight down the front of your easy-stain shirt rather than into the neck of the decanter. Funnels are usually designed with a built-in sieve to catch the finer sediment that might slip past your watchful eye. A silver one is a fabulous wedding or even engagement present for a decanter-owning wine lover. It would also make a romantic Valentine present for your other half, providing you don't think of it as just a sieve. One of these could also make a very smart christening present, one that could come in useful in later life when it comes to decanting the port the other godparent gave.

Corkscrews

Corkscrews make easy gift options at any time and are always welcome – until we get taken over by screw caps, that is. You don't even need an excuse to give a corkscrew as a present, unless it is the bank loan-requiring Leverpull (in which case a wedding is ideal, or a bosom buddy's special birthday). However attractive or hilarious the design, steer clear, like the plague, of corkscrews with the screw (or 'worm') around a central shaft, rather like a propeller. These bore a hole straight down the middle of the cork, chewing it up as they go, making its removal exceedingly tricky. You need a helix worm: a screw that's curled like a ringlet. Corkscrew designs are plentiful, and vary in usefulness and aesthetic appeal. You will know from the men you've encountered in your life that rarely do the two combine.

Useful and Ugly

The Waiter's Friend is the handiest corkscrew there is. It folds neatly away, fits easily into a pocket and comes with a built-in foil cutter and beer opener. It's a bit of an effort pulling the cork out with one of these but not back-breaking and, anyway, exercise is good for you. Downside – apart from the effort – still thinking...

The Leverpull, from Screwpull, is a cumbersome object that levers the cork out of the bottle in one slick move and then levers the cork off the screw afterwards. It's minimum effort for the lazy, tired or fragile. Downside – it's expensive, ridiculously so. Especially the designer ones that come in their own stand which you can attach to the wall (these cost upwards of £150).

Good-Looking and Useless

I love the fish corkscrew, whose mouth fits round the neck of the bottle and whose concertinaed body stretches out when you pull on the cork. This works fairly well, though you have to be careful not to catch your fingers in the sections of the fish's tummy.

I am a huge fan of simple T-shaped silver corkscrews that are made with just an elegant, modern, silver cross bar with a screw coming down from the middle. It's ludicrously difficult to pull a cork out with one of these, particularly as you have nothing to push against. Arm ache? That's not the half of it.

Naughty

In a market in Antibes, in the south of France, I found a collection of naughty corkscrews entitled Sculpteur

Sexologue. They were stick men made of scrap metal and the screw attachment was, well, you can probably guess. The artist's name is Jean Paul Mouisset at 42 Avenue Reibaud, 06600 Antibes, on 00 33 660 63 79 85.

Magic ... or is it?

Wine Wizard looks like a small telescope but is actually a neat and tidy way of removing a cork using gas (www.winewizard.uk.com). The tube fits over the neck of the bottle. One single push on the pump button on the top and the cork is pulled out under pressure. Great when it works but a pain if you run out of gas halfway up a mountain or out at sea.

Cork Spike

This is for hanging the cork around the neck of the bottle or decanter, and is particularly useful in telling you what the wine is if the bottle label has let you down or you've got two decanters on the go. Spike both ends of cork and hang the silver chain around the bottle/decanter neck. A bit like putting loo roll on a holder but more appropriate at the dinner table. A birthday gift for someone forgetful or easily confused.

Glasses

Handy devices to stop you looking like a park-bench frequenter. There's a different glass for practically every style of wine. Most break easily, so glasses make useful repeat presents for your more slippery-fingered friends. Riedel of Austria are the front-runner glass suppliers in this country with their ever-expanding, exquisitely executed lead crystal range. They make a glass for Bordeaux, younger and more mature, for Grand Cru Burgundy, for Hermitage – and so it continues. With over thirty different styles, the shapes, they say, 'are determined by the content'. The rule of thumb is this: red wines require a large glass, white wines require a medium-sized glass, and spirits or fortified wines require a small glass in order to emphasize the fruit and not the alcohol. Riedel Crystal UK (tel 020 8545 0830 or fax 020 8543 9294) have a website (www.riedelcrystal.com) where you can search for the type of glass you need according to wine/style. (They also sell decanters. Useful for the abstemious among you is the Mezzo Wine Saver: an airtight decanter for the half-bottle you just couldn't finish. You can keep opened wine for a few days this way.) Unbeatable wedding or anniversary ideas as well as a birthday present for someone special, but bear in mind that glasses can be fairly expensive and might end up being swept up sooner than you hoped.

Bottle Stoppers

To be fair, the teaspoon trick in a bottle of bubbly really does work (just don't ask me how or why). Pop one in the top and fizzy should still be fizzy three or four days later. Perhaps it isn't the most elegant device in the world. Maybe you need a bottle stopper after all: handy gifts that come in pretty presentation boxes and work for both still and sparkling wine. They make ideal presents for people you don't know very well or you don't fancy spending your life savings on – the vinous-gift equivalent of a pair of candlesticks. For your Valentine, John Lewis sell a silver-plated, heart-shaped bottle stopper. Doubt you'll have need for it, though, on Valentine's night.

Wine Coolers

Not the most refined or romantic of presents but undeniably useful, especially for a last-minute person. Bung one of these around a bottle and it will be chilled and ready to serve in about 20 minutes. Advice to the recipient: don't forget to put it back in the freezer as soon you are done with it. There is nothing more annoying than finding it warm in a drawer next time you are gasping for a glass of something cold, wet and white. My favourite is the Wine Cooler Wetsuit, which you can buy from wwwfreshtwist.co.uk. A must for any surfing buddies with a taste for wine. Available in nine different colours (hot pink does it for me), it keeps wine cool for several hours so you can take it with you to the beach.

Thermometers

For the vinous counterpart to a trainspotter, who wants to measure the exact temperature of his or her wine or to monitor the precise temperature of his or her cellar. A birthday present for someone you know to be committed to attaining perfection at all times. (See pages 93–5 for ideal temperatures for each style of wine.)

Wine Games

Bored of Trivial Pursuit, Cluedo and Uncle George's joke book at Christmas? The alternative is a wine boardgame. It's called the Wine Tasting Game, and you win points for tasting four mystery bottles of wine included in the box. Easy enough? Hold on, I haven't finished ... and for identifying the most distinctive aroma and flavour, the grape variety and the retail price, as well as answering two wine trivia questions. Think you can manage it, and all under the influence? To find out where you can get hold of it, look up www.thewinegame.com. It's definitely for a big family knees-up – guaranteed to encourage some good ol' feuding fun. Also perfect to take away on a hen weekend, when you have in mind some late-night drinking and you fancy adding a competitive dimension.

Foil Cutters

I carry a packet of plasters around at all times and for two reasons: a) I am notorious for my inability to buy shoes that fit me comfortably, and b) I never know when I am next going to cut myself trying to remove the foil from the neck of a wine bottle without the aid of a handy, pocket-fitting foil cutter. The foil cutter is a nifty gadget, with tiny tucked-away blades that when twisted across the top of the foil slice neatly through it, removing it cleanly so you can get at the cork. Such a small and inexpensive object, it's probably better to give this alongside something else wine-related. Otherwise, perfect to take to a dinner party or a friend's no-valid-reason-for-it house party, when you're not expected to take along anything at all.

Ice Buckets

Of course, a floor-mopping bucket or bath would do just as good a job of containing ice and water but it's not as elegant or mobile as some of the stunning designs for ice buckets you can find these days, particularly those dreamt up by glamorous Champagne houses. Hard-wearing ones for outdoors during the sizzling sausage season are worth looking into as well, and tend to be cheaper too. Remind the recipient to put water in along with the ice, otherwise it's very awkward to submerge the bottle(s) and it takes them much longer to cool down too. (Quick reminder: the water melts the ice and, as it does so, it draws the heat out of the bottle more quickly.) Designer ice buckets are in wedding or anniversary present territory, whereas the outdoors versions would make better gifts for a birthday barbecue or house-warming (when the host has just invested in their first garden).

Coasters

Easily done, putting a recently poured-from bottle of wine down on an antique mahogany table only to find when you pick it up that it has left a wine-stain reminder. If this was at your boss's house or during your first visit to the in-laws, you might wish you'd bought them a coaster as a 'thank you for having me' present as well.

Drip Collars

Continuing along the house-proud theme, you can stop the drop before you call on the coaster with a drip collar or wine bib. These pretty, often silver and sometimes antique objects look like napkin rings with a piece of gauze or muslin on the inside and fit round the neck of the bottle to catch the dribbles when you pour. For messy bottles that can't be relied on to mop up after themselves, and for people who prefer not to get their hands stained and sticky from trails of wine down the side of the bottle. A great gift for anyone who drinks wine. Though I have to say I think many people might not bother with it every time.

Cork Retrievers

Ever got into a fight with a stubborn cork that found you as the loser and the cork (usually in small pieces) happily bobbing about inside the bottle of wine? It's pretty hard to snake-charm the little troublemaker back out again, but that's when a cork retriever comes in handy. This twin-pronged gadget ventures inside the bottle, clasps the cork and, with a bit of luck and dexterity on the part of the user, hauls the cork back out through the neck of the bottle. A universally useful present, particularly for collectors of older wines, which often suffer from the uncomfortable complaint of cork collapse.

Wine Savers

There are many techniques for conserving wine, should you know anyone who is always on the move or who simply likes to take their time and drag out the pleasure of a treasure. The promise of one of the more recent science-lab inventions, involving nitrogen capsules, is that the wine will stay fresh for up to three weeks. I can only imagine calling on this technique myself if I'd opened something special and then found myself rushing off on an unexpected and lengthy holiday. There's the Vacuvin

Wine Sava that pumps oxygen out of the wine bottle before you put the cork back in, and the Wine Saver Spray that sprays nitrogen in through the top of the bottle. Whatever methods you use, certain changes inevitably occur in the wine. There is no better solution than to get on with sharing the bottle of wine on the day you open it.

Tastevins

Worn as medallions round the neck of pot-bellied, red-nosed French sommeliers, these were traditionally designed for people who wanted to taste wine from the barrel in a poorly lit cellar. They are shallow, silver tasting cups with circular grooves round the edge that reflect candlelight across the base of the cup so you can see how clear the wine is. A special-occasion present for someone you are confident likes spending time in dark, damp spaces. An ideal opportunity for a spot of engraving, too.

Wine Books

Books cover every aspect of wine, from the history of discovering it or the science of making it to the pleasure of drinking it or the precise soil make-up of a small vine-covered hillside in Chablis. Some are coffee-table books, some library-worthy enyclopedias and others handbag-suitable guides. Any of these makes a great birthday present for an enthusiastic wino. The less scientific or geographical publications will suit a vinous virgin who has only just taken his or her first sip. Most wine websites recommend and review books, and some will even link you up with where you can buy them.

Wine Label Library

A wine-loving stamp-collector's must-have, for keeping labels after you've enjoyed the wine. The album has spaces for sticking in the label and writing in what you thought of it and when you enjoyed it. The pack includes sticky sheets you place over the label in order to safely peel it off, which sounds unlikely but it works. For someone with more than a bottle or two and the time to peel, stick and recount their vinous exploits. A great retirement gift or birthday present for anyone who entertains a lot and wants to remember what went well with what at dinner.

Log Books and Cellar Books

For keeping track of all the treasures of the cellar. Once you have filled your storage space with the spoils of your recent spending spree, it's advisable to catalogue each wine so you know what's where and don't need to keep disturbing other wines. Typically leather-bound, these often ornate and long-lasting books make a special present for a proud cellar-owner and can be filled over the years with tasting thoughts and drinking stories.

Rent-a-Vine

Happy birthday! Here's a row of vines! One of the most original wine gift ideas around is to offer someone a share in a vineyard. Rent-a-vine is a great way to encourage understanding about the wine we drink and offers money-saving discounts. A row of vines cost £60–80 a year to rent. Go to www.latuc.com to find a château in the Cahors, Southern France, where you can rent a vine for a friend for period of at least two years, giving them the opportunity to enjoy 260 bottles a year from each row at cost price. You can even have their name printed on the label. The proprietors encourage shareholders to go out there and help tend their own vines, and also organize winter wine weekends. Your patriotic pals who don't feel the cold too badly can go grape picking at Seddlescombe organic vineyard in East Sussex instead if you offer them the opportunity to become a member of their rent-a-vine club: www.englishorganicwine.co.uk. At www.WineShare.co.uk you can find the same gift idea for vines in Provence and Bordeaux and at www.3dwines.com the choice of vines to rent ranges as widely as Burgundy, Alsace, Champagne, Bordeaux and the Rhône.

Anniversary Wines

The vintage dating on a wine bottle automatically makes it an uncannily appropriate present to mark an anniversary or birthday, retirement or corporate achievement. Wines that have survived as long as your Great-aunt Ethel are likely to be limited to red Bordeaux, port and Madeira. Still, these are some of the finest wines in the world (hence their ability to age), so she shouldn't have too much to complain about. Port, in particular, is a great christening gift, ideal for cellaring so that the naughty little ankle-biter can drink it at his or her twenty-first and probably bring it back up in a hurry the morning after – and that's if Dad hasn't stumbled home after a night at the pub and enthusiastically cracked it open before then. Here are a few companies who go all out on older vintages.

Antique Wine Company

They offer a special gift service that includes a fine wine from a chosen year with a parchment vintage report in a leather case and an engraved brass plaque with a personal message, and, what's more, a copy of *The Times* newspaper from that year as well. How's that for a trip down memory lane? Wines available date back to 1890, which should cover most of your old relatives. Antique corkscrews with space for engraving also available.

Tel 01624 824 771
Fax 01624 824 837
E-mail sales@antique-wine.com
Website www.antique-wine.com

Seckford Wines

Mature vintages going back to the 1950s. You can buy online.

Tel 01394 446 622
Fax 01394 446 633
E-mail marcus@seckfordwines.co.uk
Website www.seckfordwines.co.uk

Peter Wylie Fine Wines

Wines from classic regions, including many older vintages.
Tel 01884 277 555
E-mail peter@wylie-fine-wines.demon.co.uk
Website www.wyliefinewines.co.uk

Fine and Rare Wines

They will source what you want if they haven't already got it in their extensive list of exactly what it says in the name.
Tel 020 8960 1995
E-mail wine@frw.co.uk
Website www.frw.co.uk

Paulson Rare Wine

A German company with vintages of wine dating back to 1789. A true treasure trove waiting to be dug up and uncorked.
Website www.rare-wine.com

Engraving

Many accessory suppliers offer the opportunity to have a special message scratched in your chosen gift to make it more personal and meaningful. Particularly suitable for tastevins, coasters, drip collars (as long as you don't have much to say), a plaque on a decanter dryer or decanter base, certain corkscrews and certain ice buckets.

Stockists

This is my pick of the wine accessory stockists, with websites so you can browse from home and decide if anything is special enough for the recipient of your generosity. Most of these sites offer you the chance to buy online. A star indicates the range is a cut above the rest, offering many gift possibilities on a clear, user-friendly site.

Autour du Vin

Eurocave, the wine cabinet experts, have expanded into gifts and accessories with their new shop on Cavendish Street, London W1. Books, CDs, games, glasses, corkscrews, coolers, and more.
Tel 020 7935 4679
Fax 020 7935 0479
Website www.autourduvin.co.uk

Consort Connoisseur

Glassware, thermometers, corkscrews, coolers, decanters.

Tel 01635 550 055
Fax 01635 556 949
Website www.wine-care.co.uk

Everything but the Wine*

Everything from coasters and decanters to corkscrews and stoppers. Even corkscrew and vine cufflinks, grape earrings, corkscrew keyrings … and antique wine-related art.

Tel/fax 01869 811 027
E-mail info@everythingbutthewine.com
Website www.everythingbutthewine.com

Fraser Williamson Fine Wines

Port, wine and Champagne in gift boxes. Also wooden boxes with perfect partnerings, such as port with Stilton, Champagne with smoked salmon.

Tel 01580 200 304
Fax 01580 200 308
E-mail sales@fraserfinewines.co.uk
Website www.fraserfinewines.co.uk

The Manor House Guild

Decanter dryers, decanting machines, decanter care kits, thermometers, coasters and other paraphernalia. They sell the Bacchus Collection of wine lover's gifts.

Tel 01628 824 303
Fax 01628 826 770
E-mail manorhouse@supernet.com
Website www.wineloversgifts.com

Vacuvins

Vacuvin products include corkscrews, coolers, wine savers and wine racks.

E-mail info@vacuproducts.demon.co.uk
Website www.vacuvin.nl

Vintage Wines Ltd

Decanters, corkscrews, hip flasks, funnels, buckets, glassware, tastevins and cellar books. Engraving also available.

Tel 0115 947 6565
Fax 0115 950 5276
E-mail vintagewines@btconnect.com
Website www.vintagewinesltd.co.uk

The Waiter's Friend Company*

A thorough and imaginative range of glassware, decanters, coolers, corkscrews, wine apparel and silver-plated accessories. Ornate wine racks. Label peelers and a collector's album.

Tel 01483 560 695
Fax 01483 458 080
Website www.winegiftcentre.com

Wine Archive

Decanters, dryers and funnels, silverware, jugs, flutes.

Tel 020 8748 0968
Fax 020 8748 9880
E-mail wine_archive@ukonline.co.uk
Website www.wine-archive.com

Wineware Ltd*

Decanters, wine racks, gifts, refrigerators, corkscrews, glassware, preservation and cellarware.

Tel 01903 723 557
Fax 01903 723 557
E-mail info@wineware.co.uk
Website www.wineware.co.uk

Wineworld London*

Corkscrews, wine games, Champagne stoppers, coolers, refrigerators, racks – all from the Vinopolis gift shop at the wine centre in London.

Tel 08702 414 040
Fax 020 7940 8302
Website www.vinopolis.co.uk

York Wines

Corkscrews and gift boxes from a wine merchant.

Tel 01347 878 716
Fax 01347 878 546
E-mail sales@yorkwines.co.uk
Website www.yorkwines.co.uk

Websites

A great website selling, among other things, statues of Bacchus, the Greek god of wine, is **www.brizard. co.uk**.* Also a corkscrew collection, glasses, decanters, books, racks, and other cellar stuff. They have a link to **www. bacexpress.net** – 'for him' and 'for her' wine gifts and accessory ideas for the too lazy or too busy, personalized and sent straight to the object of your affection or appreciation.

Go to **www.sayitwithwine.co.uk** to send 'a message on a bottle'. They offer a personalized messaging service to send a thank you, a sorry or a birthday greeting to a loved one. I've always wanted to send 'How's the hangover?' They promise next-day delivery, as do **www.gifttodrink.co.uk**, who offer the same service but include a gift box with flowers if your thank you is especially heartfelt or your apology is especially grovelling ...

To satisfy the romantic in you, go to **www.giftsinternational.net** and send wine and roses or Champagne and chocolate – all with personalized greeting cards and gift packaging. Overnight in the UK or seven-day worldwide delivery.

Another favourite site is **www.drinkstuff.com** offering modern, good-looking, fun gadgety gifts. Venturing into the realm of unnecessary accessories, however, they offer Wine Finders – a pewter clip you attach to your glass so you can identify it at a party. Each has its own style so it can't be confused with anyone else's. For the hygiene-conscious. (After a few I'm not that fussed whose glass I drink from.) I love the Piranha Foil Cutter, the obvious oceanic partner to the Dolphin Bottle Opener also on the site. Order hotline – 01223 872 769.

For collectors, **www.trampsuk.com** sells funny French wine tat: antique wine baskets, old galvanized bottle carriers and other stuff you couldn't otherwise find outside a French antiques market.

And last, but by no means least, what do we women like to be given? The fact is (and there's research to back this up) women would rather be given wine than chocolates. Wine is lower-fat, more adult and more original. So if you are wondering, lads, mine's a bottle of Gigondas, if you please.

CHAPTER NINE

Laying Down

If you buy more than just the odd bottle of wine now and again, and you can resist finishing it off before you've unpacked the rest of your shopping, you might be interested in laying down wine to drink at a later date. You can lay down wine for your own curiosity, to marvel at how it stands the test of time and to savour the riches of its maturity, or you can lay down wine to witness it transform into a valuable asset that you can sell on for a princely price. Did you know that wine investment returns outperform the FTSE 100 index, Victorian paintings and gold?

Wine is a natural product, a living thing sensitive to its environment and vulnerable to spoiling, just like our delicate selves. Keeping wine from going off has been a challenge since its invention. Heat and air are the main threats: they accelerate ageing, cause the wine to referment, or simply destroy its flavour. Too much air turns wine to vinegar. The Greeks added honey to wine to preserve it, poured olive oil over the top to seal it from the air that would oxidize it, and buried it in ceramic pots in the ground to keep it cool.

In the sixteenth century wine became a valuable commodity. It was imported into this country and drunk in the place of much more harmful substances, such as…water. There was no way to stop wine oxidizing during its global travels in barrels, so much of it was fortified with brandy first. The rest was drunk as quickly as possible in the place of its making before it had time to go off.

Storing wine in the way we do now, with the added luxury of watching it transmute into something different and often more exciting, only came about with the invention of bottles and corks. In a sealed bottle, wine could be preserved for a long period of time. If wine could be laid down to become more interesting, this meant it could also become more valuable. Wine became a domain for investment, with various factors hiking up the price. Rarity is a factor. Wines hand-crafted in tiny quantities from specially selected grapes cost a great deal. The greater the demand for a limited supply, the more people will pay to get their hands on it.

The vintage

The vintage is the year in which the grapes were picked, as revealed by the date on the bottle. Nature can be cruel to the poor, vulnerable vine. In some years grapes might struggle to ripen fully, in another they might suffer sunburn. Weather plays as much of a part in the making of superb wines as does the skilful winemaker. Many of the best and most expensive wines in the world grow in marginal climates, where it's often hit or miss how they will turn out.

The date on the bottle gives the customer an insight into the level of quality to expect from the wine. To find out how a year turned out when you don't live in the region yourself and don't devote your year to studying weather patterns in the winemaking areas of the world, you can refer to vintage charts or vintage reports in websites and wine magazines. Much of the wine we drink now is made in more reliable climates, such the warm, dry sunshine of Australia or California.

Extreme vintage differences, even in the most variable

climates, are becoming less and less common as a result of technological advances. Whether it be the care and protection of a vine or the use of chemical additives to counter problems in the wine, interventions to guarantee a consistent finished product are on the increase. If we can occasionally make decent wines here in the UK with our cloudy skies and torrential rains, then good wine can be made just about anywhere, and talented winemakers now have the potential to make good wine out of poor years when once the results would have been undrinkable.

This makes overall quality more consistent, but the weather remains a powerful and unpredictable force. Some years will always be better than others, and prices are set to reflect this. Good vintages provide better investment wines: with the advantage of using better grapes, the wine has more ageing potential – the fruitiest grapes have the best balance of sugar, tannins and acidity, all of which act as preservatives. The more that has to be added artificially to a wine in the winery, the less its potential value.

Storing your wine

Only some wines have the capacity to age. Most whites and rosés are designed to be drunk as young and fresh as possible. Some white grape varieties have ageing potential, such as Riesling, Chardonnay and Semillon, for example, so long as the wines were of a sufficiently high quality in the first place. As I said above, in order to stand the test of time a wine should have generous and balanced helpings of fruit, sugar, acidity and (for red) tannins. The sugar, acidity and tannins act as preservatives. In fortified wines such as sherry, port or Madeira, alcohol is the preservative.

Should you be lucky enough to be given, or smart enough to find, a wine with ageing potential and you want to put it somewhere safe, you can use anywhere from an understairs broom cupboard to a disused fire-place to a wall in a little used spare room. You certainly don't have to live in a twelve-bedroom country manor, or spend £10,000 installing a state of-the-art, temperature- and humidity-monitoring cellar beneath your two-bed semi, in order to keep wine. Adhere to these three basic rules and you can store wine pretty much anywhere you like:

* Make sure the place you choose is cool (7–12°C), not too damp and not too dry (humidity levels somewhere between 65 and 75 per cent), and that these conditions are reasonably constant, as changes in temperature or humidity can be unsettling for wine.
* Make sure the bottle is not in direct sunlight or any other bright light.
* Make sure the bottle is lying on its side so that the cork is kept in contact with the wine (or it will shrink and possibly slip, allowing the air in to do its oxidizing damage).

The warmer the place you store wine, the faster the wine will age – prematurely – and oxidize. If it's too cold, wines will freeze, beginning with the lightest first (the higher the alcohol the longer the wine takes to freeze). When wine freezes in the bottle, the cork gets pushed out and the wine is ruined. Have you ever put a bottle in the freezer for 'express' chilling and then forgotten about it, and returned days later to find wine sorbet all over the freezer drawer?

To dampen a dry space put a wet sponge on a saucer, and don't forget to remoisten it occasionally. Insulation can help keep temperatures steady. Try to have air circulating gently, but no through hurricane if you can avoid it.

Measure your chosen space to ensure it will accommodate a single wine rack. A rack to hold fifteen bottles measures about 60cm x 25cm. If you are using an old shoe cupboard with a shoe rack, you can probably stack a couple of bottles in each section. Remember to remove bottles slowly and gently in order not to stir up the wine and disturb the forming sediment.

Put your feet up if you've got wine or port that has arrived in wooden boxes. There's no need to unpack it and rack it.

The world record price for a single bottle is $170,000 for a magnum of Château Lafite 1787, bought in 1987 by an American. He never got to try the wine, as the bottled got smashed when it was being shown off to someone. Something to think about.

Wine racks and mini cellars

Most wine racks come in self-assembly packs in set sizes. They are usually stackable and expandable, attaching to other sets of the same make to house a growing collection. Some suppliers make different sizes to accommodate magnums or funny-shaped, bulbous bottles. You can also go for made-to-measure racks. Just make sure a large rack is stable. Fix it to the wall if need be. You don't want a falling wall of valuable bottles decorating you and your surroundings.

If space is a problem but money is not, a compact but expensive solution for wine storage is the spiral cellar: a round cellar sunk into the ground below your house (sadly unsuitable for most people in flats) and entered by an integral spiral stair. Bottles are stored in a honeycomb of bins that make up the outer wall of the cellar.

You can also buy free-standing, thermostatically controlled cabinets capable of housing upwards of fifty bottles. The most sophisticated of these, the Eurothèque, has three temperature zones: a room-temperature section on top to warm up a 'cellared' red wine ready for drinking; a cellar-temperature section in the middle for all the wines you can keep your hands off, and a chilled section on the bottom to get your bubbly or your white wine primed for your imminent guests. Eurocave are the best company for these (see below).

Rack suppliers

Here are the major suppliers. They sell other wine accessories as well. Have a look at what they've got on their websites or ring for a brochure.

Bordex Wine Racks

Tel 01245 320 141
Fax 01245 323 972
E-mail Douglasgreen@bordex.co.uk
Website www.bordex.co.uk

K. Colombier

Tel 01753 889 339
Fax 01753 885 513
E-mail sales@finewineuk.com
Website www.finewineuk.com

Eurocave Importers

Tel 020 7935 4679
Fax 020 7935 0479
E-mail admin@eurocave.co.uk
Website www.eurocave.co.uk

Great Western Wine Company

Tel 01225 322 800
Fax 01225 442 139
Website www.greatwesternwine.co.uk

A and W Moore Wine Rack Company

Tel 0115 944 1434
Fax 0115 932 0735
Website www.wineracks.co.uk

Sorrells Wine Racks

Tel 01243 543 253
Fax 01243 543 253
Website www.sorrells-wineracks.co.uk

Spiral Cellars

Tel 01372 279 166
Fax 01372 273 482
E-mail info@spiralcellars.free-online.co.uk
Website www.spiralcellars.com

Wineware (Racks and Accessories)

Tel 01903 723 557
Fax 01903 723 557
E-mail info@wineware.co.uk
Website www.wineware.co.uk

York Wines

Tel 01347 878 716
Fax 01347 878 546
E-mail sales@yorkwines.co.uk
Website www.yorkwines.co.uk

Monitoring your wine

Once in place, does your wine need constant attention like a demanding child, or is it best left to make its journey into adulthood alone, as most teenagers would like to be?

Most wine doesn't need permanent monitoring. It isn't going to get up to much from its comfortable horizontal position in storage. Watching your gloss topcoat drying is more likely to offer visual stimulation. You should, however, check on the wines every few months to see that the labels are not rotting from damp (see below for how to look after labels), or that the cork hasn't dried up or slipped in an old bottle that's missing its foil or wax seal, letting air in and wine out (think how frustrated you would be to find a half-empty bottle of your most treasured investment).

Keep a wine log book, and use numbered or named cards on each row or rack to refer you to the relevant log book entry (so you don't have to keep disturbing the bottles to remind you what's what). Remember not to leave the log book in an area that's damp. Log books also provide space for you to write down what you think of the wines as and when you drink them, which is particularly worthwhile if you are trying bottles from the same case over a number of years and want to see how they change. These days it is probably more efficient, though less romantic, to keep a log of your wines on a computer database. You can sort them any way you like and it's easy to update.

Do make sure no bored adolescents or practical joke experts think it would be funny to steal into your storage in the dead of night and rearrange your diligently logged layout. Keep it locked if you believe yourself to be in a high-risk category.

Label care

Looking after the label on the bottle is almost as important as preserving the wine inside. A light dusting of mould on the label and a little fraying around its edges can give a bottle character and kudos, but if the label becomes illegible or falls off it won't do you any good at all, even if you are an expert in blind-tasting by then. Hairspray is one answer. Pick the least scented one you can find, and spray it over labels to keep them fresh. Otherwise wrap clingfilm around the bottle from the shoulders downwards (leave the foil free so the closure end can breathe). This keeps damp away and protects against leakages from above.

If you are keen for a new gizmo, how about plastic seals for the crossbars of a metal rack to ensure smooth bottle removal and no label scratching? Clipco sell them in bulk (tel 01245 323 388; e-mail info@clipco.co.uk). If you must.

Choosing what to lay down

Now the fun really begins. Wine merchants and wine brokers can advise you on what to buy to lay down and which wines might make you money. Some even offer 'ready-made cellars'. Great if you're a beginner but a bit boring once you've got some knowledge and preferences of your own. After all, only you can decide exactly which wines you like and which ones you want to wait for. It would be as pointless for me to dictate the contents of your cellar as it would be for me to tell you what food to put in your fridge and what clothes to put in your wardrobe. But I can tell you what's in the running. Only certain countries, regions and styles of wine are built to last and are potentially palm-sweatingly valuable to make you filthy rich. Here are some of the possibilities, with wine or producer names where applicable.

Bordeaux

Wines from the region of Bordeaux deserve their own special introduction since they make the most hefty contribution to the world auction market. Since the twelfth century and the marriage of Eleanor of Aquitaine and Henry Plantagenet (future king of England), links between England and Gascony ensured that Bordeaux wines were cheap as chips for the English to import. This finally went belly-up during the Anglo-French wars in the eighteenth century, but still Bordeaux wines reached English shores (mostly smuggled). They were top of the pops at Christie's first auctions in 1766, and so London became a clearing-house for fine French wine. More recently, fine wines became a fashionable accessory for Americans as well. Market prices these days are driven largely by the pen-power of one man, Robert Parker, who writes for *The Wine Advocate* in the States. Prices rise and fall according to his comments and marks out of a hundred. Other winemaking countries, such as Italy, Australia, Spain and the US, have begun to make wines that Parker also wants to curl up on the sofa with, and their prices are beginning to rise accordingly. I look forward to a woman, other than Madonna, having this scale of influence one day.

The kind, mild climate, the influence of the windy Atlantic, the well-draining soils that don't waterlog and the clever combination of appropriate grape varieties – all ensure that the best Bordeaux wines have the quality and the ability to withstand the test of time. These are some of the names to look for:

Médoc

Château Lafite, Latour, Margaux, Mouton-Rothschild, Brane-Cantenac, Lascombes, Léoville-Barton, Léoville-Las-Cases, Pichon-Baron, Pichon-Lalande, Ducru-Beaucaillou, Cos d'Estournel, Montrose, Gruaud-Larose, Rausan-Ségla, Palmer, Lynch-Bages, Chasse-Spleen, Les Ormes de Pez, Cantemerle, Calon-Ségur, Beychevelle, Talbot, Siran

Graves / Pessac-Léognan

Domaine de Chevalier, Château la Louvière, Haut-Bailly, Fieuzal, Haut-Brion

St-Émilion

Château Ausone, Pavie, Figeac, Cheval-Blanc, Canon, Trottevielle, L'Angelus, Troplong Mondot

Pomerol

Château Pétrus, Lafleur, Le Pin, L'Evangile, Vieux-Château-Certan, Certan-de-May, Trotanoy, Clinet, de Valandraud

Sauternes / Barsac

Château d'Yquem, Rieussec, Coutet, Climens

Everywhere Else: Old World

It's not *all* about Bordeaux, of course.

Burgundy

Domaine de la Romanée Conti, Meo-Camuzet, D. Rion et Fils, M. Lafarge, Leflaive, Lafon, Leroy, Joseph Drouhin, Ramonet, Verget, Etienne Sauzet, Armand Rousseau, Trapet

Rhône

Guigal, Jaboulet Ainé, Château du Beaucastel, Chapoutier, Cuilleron, Vernay, Vieux Telegraphe

Germany

Egon Müller, Fritz Hagg, Joh Jos Prum, Selbach-Oster, Kurt Darting, Muller-Catoir, Balthasar Ress, Dr Bürklin-Wolf, von Schubert, Bassermann-Jordan, H. J. Ernst

Spain

Vega Sicilia, Pesquera, Marques de Riscal, Jean Leon, Torres Mas la Plana

Italy

Gaja, Ornellia, Marchesi Incisa della Rocchetta (Sassicaia), Castello di Ama, Prunotto (Barolo), Marchesi di Frescobaldi, Antinori (Tignanello), Paulo Scavino, Vasco Sassetti, Ca'del Bosco, Castelgiocondo (Brunello)

Champagne

Dom Perignon, Krug, Roederer Cristal, Pol Roger Cuvée Winston Churchill, Bollinger Grand Année, Salon Le Mesnil, Taittinger Comtes de Champagne, Pommery Louise, Billecart-Salmon Cuvée F Billecart

Port

Taylor's, Graham's, Dow's, Niepoort, Noval, Quinta do Crasto, Quinta du Vesuvio, Churchill, Croft (Roeda), Sandeman

Sherry

Hidalgo, Emilio Lustau, Gonzalez Byass, Pedro Domecq, Barbadillo, Osborne y Ca

Madeira

Blandy's, Henriques and Henriques, Justino Henriques

New World

The New World of wine is exactly that to the investment industry: new. Many countries or regions don't have wines or even vines old enough to compete with the tradition of Europe, but an increasing number of star performers are making wines with serious laying-down potential, now reaching cult status at wallet-stretching prices (much of it thanks to Robert Parker). Here are some of the names I think you should be taking seriously.

Australia

Penfolds Grange, Henschke, Coldstream Hills, Petaluma, Leeuwin Estate, Yarra Yerring, Cullens, Woodstock

USA

Phelps, Bonny Doon, Saintsbury, Au Bon Climat, Ridge Vineyards, Knappstein, Simi, Chalone, Andrew Will, Amity Vineyards, Domaine Drouhin, Duckhorn, Frogs Leap, Opus One, Swanson, Dominus

South Africa

Hamilton Russell, Thelema, Nederburg

New Zealand

Martinborough Vineyards, Cloudy Bay, Kumeu River, Church Road, Dry River

South America

Casa Lapostelle Cuvée Alexandre, Concha Y Toro Don Melchor

Where do you buy these wines?

Fine wine merchants and brokers will help you find the wines you are looking for. Most also offer certain wines 'en primeur' (the Americans call it 'futures'), which means ordering a wine up to two years before it is even on the market because industry prediction (or Robert Parker) says it is going to be worth it – that is, the vintage was a success, the producer has a reliable reputation and the demand will be high. You pay cash in advance, which will be less than its predicted eventual release price.

Be aware that some of the most expensive and highly sought-after wines in the world are very difficult to get hold of unless you can infiltrate the tight sales loop. A limited number of cases of a wine like Château Pétrus, for example (worth between £3,000 and £15,000 a case, depending on the vintage) are allocated to an importer, who offers the wine to a select group of wholesalers, who pass it on to their select group of wine shops and restaurants, chosen for their past sales success records. The wine merchant offers the wine to regular collectors whom they can rely on to buy it every year whatever the cost. Break into that as a first-time buyer if you can.

Don't be disheartened. If you are just starting a collection I wouldn't recommend you to go straight for the vinous jugular anyway. Try to find wines that have potential but which you don't have to beg, borrow or rob people for. It's easier to get to the big stuff if you build up a good relationship with a broker or merchant first anyway.

If you are buying a large quantity for investment that you are unable to cellar yourself, you can have them held in bond for you by a reliable merchant as they do their growing up. Five years is a general minimum recommended investment period.

Imagine you find tucked away in a dark corner of your damp basement a case of wine you bought in a supermarket on your honeymoon to Nice or on a French study outing to Boulogne-sur-Mer. You've just been reliably informed it is worth a small fortune. What do you do with it? One option is to sell it to your fine wine merchant, who will either pay cash or set up a brokerage deal, in other words, find a buyer for you but take a percentage. Other options include the internet and auction houses, of which more below.

Why invest?

* On average you can see over 12 per cent increase per year over a period of investment of ten years.
* Any profits are capital gains tax free.
* Wine investment outperforms many other investment markets.
* You have the guarantee of wines to drink even if your investment drops in value or there's a crash. Can't get that promise from share certificates under the same circumstances.

Investment trust

Not that I wish to make wine-investing sound like the plot of a James Bond movie, but, as with art, there is a certain scope for bogus business. Some unscrupulous brokers prey on the potential inexperience of investors, particularly women, where it is assumed that wine and money are two subjects the 'fairer sex' couldn't possibly understand. If you are worried about being stung or you feel your projected price promise is too good to be true, you can get advice from www.investdrinks.org, a website dedicated to showing the dangers of wine investment, and offering advice and the names of trustworthy brokers, merchants and auction houses. Otherwise there is *Decanter*'s Fine Wine Tracker (www.decanter.com), which is free and follows the latest auction prices and trends. It will tell you how much up to 2,500 different wines are worth as well as help you create your own personal wine portfolio and keep track of its value with their automatic cellar valuation service.

When investing in wine take the following commonsense precautions.

* Make enquiries into the wine and who is selling it.
* Don't rush into making a decision on what you are going to buy.
* Only purchase whole original cases over the internet if you are quite certain you can trust the merchant.
* Compare what other merchants are offering or what other companies' predicted value increases are for the same wines.
* Check out your rights to cancel or return.
* Check that the wines are being offered in their original cases and in good condition. If you are buying less than a case at a time, try to ensure that you actually see the bottles.
* Last but not least, wear an armour-plated vest and tell a friend where you are going if asked to meet a strange man to discuss a large investment in a secluded warehouse in Dagenham.

Drinking up or selling on

How do you know if a wine is ready to drink or to sell on? Wines change at different rates according to the way they are made and the way they are stored, so it's a bit like asking how long is a piece of string. Red wine, the most commonly cellared style, will go from being a tight, young and toughly tannic teenager to a softer, more complex, mature adult with new aromas and more layers of flavour as the result of chemical reactions inside the bottle. At a certain point it has a mid-life crisis, where it might become 'dumb' and lose a lot of its character. This doesn't last, but rather marks the final moment of growing up before maturity. Maturity doesn't last for ever, either, and wine can go 'past it' or 'over the hill'. The basic principle is that the tighter and more structured a wine is at the beginning, the greater its life expectancy. It is often worth trying a bottle of the wine you wish to lay down to see how much potential it appears to have. Alternatively, of course, you can trust the advice of those who are selling it to you, or that of an impartial, knowledgeable wine expert.

Wine Merchants

To get you started, here's my pick of reliable merchants, all with websites where you can buy online.

L'Assemblage Fine Wine Traders

Easy to use, attractive website with comprehensive list.
Tel 020 8876 0300
Fax 020 8392 0810
E-mail sales@lassemblage.co.uk
Website www.lassemblage.co.uk

Berry Bros and Rudd

Three-hundred-year-old merchants. Top-end wines, cellaring/broking advice and information.
Tel 020 7396 9600
Fax 020 7396 9611
E-mail orders@bbr.com
Website www.bbr.co.uk

Bordeaux Index

Bordeaux (of course), Burgundy and Italy their best. Free valuation service.
Tel 020 7253 2110
Fax 020 7490 1955
E-mail sales@bordeauxindex.com
Website www.bordeauxindex.com

Cave Cru Classé

Slightly thin site but good wines at all prices.
Tel 020 7378 8579
Fax 020 7378 8544
E-mail enquiries@ccc.co.uk
Website www.cave-cru-classe.com

Claret-e

Slick, modern website with fine and everyday wines and investment guidance.

Tel 020 7736 7658
Fax 020 7384 9535
Website www.claret-e.com

Corney and Barrow

Long-established fine wine merchant with top-notch broking division.

Tel 020 7539 3200
Fax 020 7608 2234
E-mail wine@corbar.co.uk
Website www.corneyandbarrow.com

Farr Vintners

Biggest Bordeaux wholesalers in the country; also sell to private customers at a minimum order of £500. Supply and stock many other countries' wines as well.

Tel 020 7821 2000
Fax 020 7821 2020
E-mail sales@farr-vintners.com
Website www.farrvintners.com

Fine and Rare Wines

Specialists in just that. Online brokers.

Tel 020 8960 1995
Fax 020 8960 1911
E-mail wine@frw.co.uk
Website www.frw.co.uk

Lay and Wheeler

Extensive list, packed website, including Cellar Plan – where they select wines for you to lay down and you spread your payments over monthly instalments. Bit like buying a car or TV but hopefully a better investment.

Tel 01206 764 446
Fax 01206 560 002
E-mail sales@laywheeler.com
Website www.laywheeler.com

Magnum Fine Wines

Drinking wines and investing wines clearly divided. Good investment advice.

Tel 020 7839 5732
Fax 020 7321 0848
E-mail wine@magnum.co.uk
Website www.magnum.co.uk

Seckford Wines

Broad range, specializing in fine and rare wines, particularly older vintages. Detailed search facility on website.

Tel 01394 446 622

Fax 01394 446 633

E-mail marcus@seckfordwines.co.uk

Website www.seckfordwines.co.uk

Uvine

A global exchange, wine marketplace and membership site for buying and selling wine on the internet.

E-mail enquiries@uvine.com

Website www.uvine.com

www.wine-owners.com

An online-only membership site offering free personal wine cellar software that allows you to keep track of your wine collection and create a history of your drinking preferences. You can also share tasting notes and reviews, value fine wine, and buy from leading wine merchants and collectors. You can sell wine here too.

Going once... Going twice...

There may have been a time when women found wine auctions intimidating arenas monopolized by nose-scratching, know-it-all men. Not any more. Raised female arms and paddles are nearly as commonplace as men's now. And Sotheby's Auction Wine Department, with its great heritage, is run by a woman, Serena Sutcliffe MW.

Ask for a programme of forthcoming auctions and you can see what's going to be on offer. The description of each wine should include details of the condition of the bottles (such as decayed labels). If you want to attend you must turn up 20 to 30 minutes before the bidding begins so that you can collect your bidding paddle and register your details (name, address, contact number and in some cases your bank or credit information). Most auction houses are open for viewing on the day of the auction a few hours before it starts. The first time you bid you will be given a client number. You do not need to book or buy tickets to attend most auctions. If you cannot make it to the auction, you can enter an absentee bid in advance or over the telephone during the bidding.

If you wish to sell you should contact the auction house first and find out whether you need to arrange an inspection of the wine and whether they can give you an estimate. Estimates can take four to six weeks, so plan ahead and find out when the next auction is happening in your area. When the wine has been sold you can either arrange yourself for the wine to be delivered or ask the auction house to arrange it.

Auctioneers

Here are some of the major auctioneers. Note that most websites only list lot information for forthcoming auctions a few weeks before the event.

Bigwood Auctioneers Ltd, Stratford-upon-Avon

Affordable prices; short list but most countries included.
Tel 01789 269 415
Fax 01789 294 168

Bonhams, London

Bordeaux and Burgundy mostly but some Italy, Germany, Champagne and ports. Wine is just one of many things they auction.
Tel 020 7393 3900
Fax 020 7393 3906
Website www.bonhams.com

Christie's, London

Mainly Bordeaux but also Burgundy, Champagne, Rhône, Tuscany, Spain, Germany, California. Founded in 1766, the great auction house of England offers many other items besides wine.
Tel 020 7839 9060
Fax 020 7839 1611
Website www.christies.com

Dreweatt Neate, Newbury

Short list but wide reaching, many countries represented. Look for wine under 'Fine Art'.
Tel 01635 553 553
Fax 01635 553 599
Website www.auctions.dreweatt-neate.co.uk

Morphets Auction House, Harrogate

Mainly fine wines, ports and Champagne. Twice-a-year wine sales.
Tel 01423 530 030
Fax 01423 500 717
Website www.morphets.co.uk

Sotheby's, London

Plenty of Bordeaux, increasing Burgundy and others. One wine auction a month; much else on auction too.
Tel 020 7293 6423
Fax 020 7293 5961
Website www.sothebys.com

J. Straker, Chadwick and Sons, Abergavenny

Six to seven wine auctions a year covering a good range of countries, from this long-established land and property auctioneers.
Tel 01873 852 624
Fax 01873 857 311
Website www.strakerchadwick.co.uk

Winebid.com

Online auctioning, from single bottles to case lots.
E-mail glang@winebid.com
Website www.winebid.com

Expanding Your Wine Learning

Is buying wine increasing your thirst for knowledge on the subject? Do you want to be an informed buyer or investor or just accept what's recommended by wine buffs or brokers who want to make money out of you? If you ache to be a wine geek and indulge your classroom fantasies, there are many ways of learning more about wine these days: you've made a start just by reading this book. You can take courses in wine, and even take exams if you want to. The courses are co-educational, men and women grown up enough to study and taste wine in the same room without misbehaving. If you are currently unattached, it might even be a way of encountering a new, like-minded, wine-fuelled love interest.

Association of Wine Educators

This association has an extremely useful list of all the wine educators in the country.

Tel 020 8931 1128
Fax 020 8958 3319
E-mail admin@wineeducators.com
Website www.wineeducators.com

Christie's Wine Course

Courses held throughout the year. Introduction To Wine Tasting is the most popular, held over five weeks, seven times a year. Can arrange seminars abroad too.

Tel 020 7747 6800
Fax 020 7747 6801
E-mail education@christies.com
Website www.christies.com

Connoisseur

Tastings and courses for all levels in a relaxed atmosphere. Strong on participation and discussion, i.e. drinking and chatting. Two-hour sessions in central London over courses of five to six weeks.

Tel 020 7328 2448
Fax 020 7681 9905
E-mail tastings@connoisseur.org
Website www.connoisseur.org

Grapesense

Wine for beginners, wine appreciation and WSET (Wine and Spirit Education Trust) courses available in Bury St Edmunds and Cambridge.

Tel 01359 270 318
Fax 01359 270 318
E-mail grapesense@aol.com
Website www.grapesense.com

Leith's School of Food and Wine

Extensive wine and food courses for all levels in London. Informal and weekly evening courses. You can take Leith's Certificate in Wine if you want something to show for it. They run Wine and Food Matching evenings too.

Tel 020 7229 0177
E-mail info@leiths.com
Website www.leiths.com

London Wine Academy Ltd

Good choice of courses for all levels in London, bookable online.

Tel 08701 000 100
E-mail info@LondonWineAcademy.com
Website www.londonwineacademy.com

Plumpton College

WSET (see below) courses and general interest in wine. You can do an HND in Wine Studies here if you are superkeen or feel you have a vinous vocation. The college has its own commercial vineyard and winery on site.

Tel 01273 890 454
Fax 01273 890 071
E-mail staff@plumpton.ac.uk
Website www.plumpton.ac.uk

The Wine and Spirit Education Trust

WSET courses and qualifications, particularly relevant if you already work in wine or are interested in doing so. Informative website. Over 170 centres nationwide.

Tel 020 7236 3551
Fax 020 7329 8712
E-mail wset@wset.co.uk
Website www.wset.co.uk

Wine Education Service

Extensive wine courses for all levels with centres in London, Birmingham and Manchester.

Tel 020 8423 6338
E-mail info@wine-education-service.co.uk
Website www.wine-education-service.co.uk

Wine and Food Academy

The Fame of food and wine. Good courses especially for the wine novice. Also offer wine trips abroad.

Tel 020 8675 6172
Fax 020 8675 9781
E-mail louise@winefoodacademy.com
Website www.winefoodacademy.com

Young's Courses

This brewery takes their wine very seriously. Their courses are held in pubs around the country and range in topic from An Introduction to Wine, Food and Wine Matching, Champagne vs Sparkling Wine and New World vs Old World. They are fun, relaxed and informative and often attract a younger crowd.

Tel 020 8875 7008
Fax 020 8875 7009
E-mail clare.young@youngs.co.uk
Website www.youngswinedirect.co.uk

The Wine Tutor

If you don't like the classrooms or going to school after work seems too weird to you or is too expensive, you can study wine from the comfort of your house with the Wine Tutor, an at-home wine course designed by Blue Tree Ltd. *A Practical Introduction to Wine* is for a vinous amateur and includes nine half-bottles of wine, six audio CDs, a course book, a support book (with the answers to quiz questions so don't cheat!) and the assignment of a wine tutor who can be contacted by e-mail. On sale at www.everywine.co.uk, or ring 020 7751 0814 for more information.

Wine Clubs

Does the mere thought fill you with dread? A room full of bespectacled bores reciting vintage charts? Clubs can be much more fun than that, I promise you, and if you get a group of friends to go along then you know you'll be in good company, enjoying fine wine and often good grub too. Many clubs are run by wine merchants who want to introduce local people to their wine lists, so it's a good way to try new wines you might then want to buy. Here's a list of clubs and societies worth getting involved in (all with websites), and also websites that show you where to find other clubs local to you. They vary from small groups in village halls with cheese and biscuits at half-time and enthusiastic guest speakers, to wine merchants offering club membership benefits and incentives.

Barrels and Bottles

Tastings and dinners for customers.
Tel 0114 255 6611
Fax 0114 255 1010
E-mail tastings@barrelsandbottles.co.uk
Website www.barrelsandbottles.co.uk

Corney and Barrow (Scotland)

Discounts, quarterly newsletters and tastings.
Tel 01292 267 000
Fax 01292 265 903
E-mail enquiries@corbar1.demon.co.uk
Website www.corneyandbarrow.com/2002/scotland

Dulwich Wine Society

Weekly evening meetings.
Tel 020 8699 4742
Fax 020 8265 5493
E-mail dws@havenhand.cix.co.uk
Website www.dulwich-wine-society.co.uk

East Coast Wine Ltd

Private members club with bi-annual tastings.
Tel 01507 363 525
Fax 01507 363 529
E-mail sales@eastcoastwine.co.uk
Website www.eastcoastwine.co.uk

International Wine Clubs Association

Thirty-six member companies in eighteen countries.
Tel 01923 210 508
Fax 01923 444 798
E-mail info@internationalwineclubs.com
Website www.internationalwineclubs.com

International Wine and Food Society

International society offering details of tastings, events and vineyard visits. Benefits include restaurant, hotel and event discounts.
Tel 020 7495 4191
Fax 020 7495 4172
E-mail sec@iwfs.com
Website www.iwfs.com.

Magnum Fine Wines

Newsletters, wine tastings and vintage information.
Tel 020 7839 5732
Fax 020 7321 0848
E-mail wine@magnum.co.uk
Website www.magnum.co.uk

North Hampshire Wine Society

Monthly meetings and tastings in Basingstoke.
Tel 01256 328 180
E-mail secretary@north-hampshire-wine-society.org.uk
Website www.north-hampshire-wine-society.org.uk

Rioja Wine Club

If you are Rioja potty, this specialist buying club is for you. Free membership with first order. Newsletters and information on trips.

E-mail riojawineclub@aol.com

Website www.riojawineclub.co.uk

Royton Wine Society

Monthly meetings and tastings, often with a guest speaker.

Tel 0161 620 9446

E-mail etchelli@aol.com

Website www.users.waitrose.com/~roytonwine

Scottish Amateur Winemakers

Into home brewing? An organizing body for winemaking circles and home-brewing clubs in Scotland.

E-mail peter@wineart.freeserve.co.uk

Website www.scottishamateurwinemakers.co.uk

Sunday Times Wine Club

See Wine Tours, facing page.

Tanglewood Wine Society/Tours

See Wine Tours, facing page.

Veralum Wine Tasting Club

Nine meetings a year in St Albans. Regular guest speakers in the profession.

Tel 01438 714 873

E-mail info@vwtc.org

Website www.vwtc.org

Wine Share Ltd

A club that offers you the chance to own a vine yourself, visit the winery and buy the results (see page 196).

Tel 01306 742 164

Fax 01306 743 936

E-mail enquiries@wineshare.co.uk

Website www.wineshare.co.uk

Wine on the Web

An extensive directory of clubs and societies throughout the country. Find your local meeting place here, as well as lots of other information.

Website www.wineontheweb.co.uk

The Wine Society

£40 a year for membership of this cooperative mail-order-only company. Offers access to members' reserve cellar and regular tastings.

Tel 01438 740 222
Fax 01438 761 167
E-mail membersservices@thewinesociety.com
Website www.the winesociety.com

Wine Tours

It's all very well staring at a glass of wine against a sheet of white paper at a desk in a brightly lit classroom, or sitting round a dining table debating the merits of oak usage, but there is no better way to appreciate and to understand wine than to visit the places where it is made. An increasing number of wine tours and travel itineraries can take you to the heart of wine-growing regions where you can wander through the vines, taste the grapes as they grow, speak to the people who make the wine and try it straight from the tank or barrel. Being knee-deep in a vat or hosed down with a winery pipe is certain to increase your thirst and enthusiasm for wine. Tours are a good choice for a holiday with your other half. Or bulk-book for a group of friends and maybe have a tour tailor-made for you. Go on. Get your hands and feet dirty.

Arblaster and Clarke Wine Tours Ltd

Market leaders for organized tours all over the winemaking world. Led by knowledgeable and enthusiastic wine guides. They also offer walking tours through France and private tours to suit all tastes and perversions.

Tel 01730 893 344
Fax 01730 892 888
E-mail sales@winetours.co.uk
Website www.arblasterandclarke.com

Denbies

South-east England vineyard open to public for tours and tasting. Be patriotic and go along for the day.

Tel 01306 742 224
Website www.denbiesvineyard.co.uk

French Wine Tours Direct

Well-structured tours in France. Customer feedback on website.

Tel 01291 690 231

E-mail optima.mcandrew@virgin.net

Website www.winetours-france.com

Jon Hurley's Wine Weekends

Something for the weekend, sir/madam? Country-house breaks with a wine theme.

Tel 01432 840 649

E-mail enquiries@wineweekends.com

Website www.wineweekends.com

Sunday Times Wine Club Tours

Worldwide wine tours for club members, catering for all needs. A hen weekend to Champagne sound like the thing for you? All from the leading mail-order wine club with membership benefits.

Tel 01730 895 353

Fax 01730 892 888

E-mail clubtours@winetours.co.uk

Website www.sundaytimeswineclub.co.uk.

Tanglewood Wine

Extensive wine coach tours of Europe and California run by husband and wife team Jean and John Trigwell. For all levels of wine interest, and including other sightseeing, leisure activities and shopping too. Regular meetings for club members.

Tel 01932 348 720

Fax 01932 350 861

E-mail jean@tanglewoodwine.co.uk

Website www.tanglewoodwine.co.uk.

Vallicorte

Food and wine tours in Italy.

Tel 020 7680 1377

E-mail tours@vallicorte.com

Website www.vallicorte.com

Winetrails

Excellent website. Extensive, well-organized tours worldwide with the focus as much on fine food, walking, cycling, art, history and nature as wine.

Tel 01306 712 111

Fax 01306 713 504

E-mail sales@winetrails.co.uk

Website www.winetrails.co.uk

The Wine and Travel Company

Small private guided groups or customized tours of wine regions in Spain, Australia, NZ, Hungary and Canada. Suitable for the non-wine-obsessive too.

E-mail info@thewineandtravelco.com
Website www.thewineandtravelco.com

Website Wine Learning

There are, doubtless, those of you who want to know more about wine but from the comfort of your own chair. To expand your mind without shrinking your wallet, travel no further than the following websites … whether to understand more about how wine is made, read tasting notes on certain wines, find out about particular vintages, read reviews of bars, restaurants or wine books, or get investment and auction information – all this and more. Some have wine book link-ups as well and can connect you straight to other sites too.

www.thewinedoctor.com
general reference and wide-reaching wine information

www.decanter.com
the magazine online, and more

www.thewine-pages.com
good resource for wine information, including vintage charts, quizzes and book reviews; hosts the wine forum; see below

www.ukwineforum.com
a site for topical discussions

www.wineanorak.com
well designed, stimulating, frequently updated, with a helpful, light-hearted 'new to wine' section

www.jancisrobinson.com
personal opinion and recommendations from the guru Jancis; you need to subscribe to visit

www.superplonk.com
Malcolm Gluck's guide to good cheap drinking; handy search option for recommendations from specific wine stores

www.winespectator.com
US website of magazine, subscribers only; detailed and thorough

www.winepros.com
Australian information site

www.winefocus.com
lists of wine websites, based in the US

www.wineoftheweek.com
and much more, on this New Zealand site

www.DamnGoodWine.com
in-depth wine reviews, wine Q&A, information, articles and much more, all with a young, fun approach.

Oh yes, there are many more than these chosen few. New ones come on board and others fall off every week.

CHAPTER TEN

To Your Health

In vino sanitas

In wine there is health

PLINY THE ELDER, AD 23–79,
SOLDIER, SCIENTIST AND HISTORIAN

'A GLASS OF WINE A DAY KEEPS THE DOCTOR AT BAY.' THE ISSUE of wine and health is heavily researched, much debated and bullet-holed with contradictions. Wine is a form of alcohol, the addictive drug in which our culture is quite literally marinated. Alcohol is responsible for over 30,000 deaths a year in the UK alone. One in six of us has a serious hangover a couple of times a month. (Is that all?) On the other hand, you can argue, and with good reason, that drinking wine in moderation can enrich and improve our lives while increasing our valuable time on this precious earth. As Dr Phillip Norrie, the Australian physician, wine and medical historian, says, 'Wine can help you die young as late as possible.'

The discovery of the medicinal benefits of wine are not exactly original – you only have to look at historical accounts to see that wine has been employed and enjoyed by the medical profession for thousands of years. The Ancient Egyptians used it as a solvent for mixing their medicinal potions. The oldest known medical handbook, a clay tablet found in the area we now know as Iraq, recommends mixing sweet wine with honey to treat coughing. The Bible tells us that the Hebrews treasured wine for its valuable antiseptic qualities, and used it to wash the wounds of circumcision.

The Ancient Greeks simply couldn't live without it. The most famous of ancient physicians, Hippocrates, in his medical text *Regiment* suggested using wine 'as a wound dressing, as a nourishing dietary beverage, as a cooling agent for fevers, as a purgative and as a diuretic'. In the great epics, the *Iliad* and the *Odyssey*, wine is described as an antiseptic and a sedative.

Galen, doctor to Roman gladiators, recommended wine-soaked bandages to treat their worst wounds. Wine was mixed with medicinal plants to make them bearable to ingest. Julius Caesar recommended wine for his soldiers for their 'strength, good health and to prevent dysentery'.

So it continued into the Middle Ages, when medical care was largely in the hands of religious orders. Thankfully the sick did not rely on the quality of the wine (winemaking standards were at a low point) but merely on its benefits in the treatment of wounds and infections.

In 1773 the single biggest expenditure of Leicester hospital was on wine for the patients. During the eighteenth and nineteenth centuries wine was used on board ships to prevent scurvy. On convict ships it was found to be particularly useful in fending off 'gaol fever' (typhus). Wine was preferred over water; it was safer than water, too.

In nineteenth-century Australia, three doctors founded wineries that were to become among the most important in the modern Australian wine industry: Penfolds, Hardy's and Lindemann's.

And so to the twenty-first century, and a time when we know, or think we know, more than ever about the beneficial and harmful effects of drinking wine. One thing is clear: wine will continue to be a subject of long debate. On the one hand it is heralded as preventative medicine, and on the other derided as a dangerous substance capable of destroying lives.

It goes against my instincts to detail the potentially damaging effects of alcohol in a book written to celebrate the joys of wine. However, I don't think it would be right to paint a bright and colourful picture without filling in some of the shade. As you read on, remember that most of the gruesome stuff applies to alcohol being consumed in excess. As long ago as the fifteenth century, Paracelsus (1493–1541), a German physician and the alleged father of modern pharmacology, had worked out: 'Whether wine is a medicine, nourishment or poison, it is a matter of dosage.' Moderate consumption, or 'sensible drinking' as it has been commonly termed, is not proven to have the same deleterious effects as drinking too much – although, of course, one person's moderation is another person's excess.

Wine contains water, alcohol, sugar, acids and antioxidants. It is the antioxidants and alcohol that both benefit us the most and cause us the greatest concern. Alcohol may be responsible for getting you in the mood for loving, but evidence has shown that antioxidants are physically good for your heart (and much more besides). Wine also contains vitamins, minerals, trace elements and amino acids, all of which can act as a valuable tonic.

The downside of alcohol

Are you ready? You are not going to like this. The alcohol in wine can damage the liver, stomach, oesophagus, pancreas, brain and nervous system, bones, muscles, skin and sex organs. It disturbs sleep and can make people unhappy and angry. It can also be responsible for certain cancers.

The liver is a major trouble spot. This is where the

body filters and breaks down the alcohol we consume. If given too much to do, it becomes damaged. The worst case is cirrhosis of the liver, when it is no longer able to repair itself and for which there is no cure. This affects 10–30 per cent of heavy drinkers.

Heavy drinkers may develop an inflamed pancreas too, as well as high blood pressure, which increases their chances of suffering a stroke. Heavy drinking can contribute to osteoporosis: thinning and softening of the bones. It can increase the severity of gout: a painful swelling of the joints. Muscles might be weakened. The skin might be affected by the development or worsening of psoriasis, eczema or patchy redness (rosacea). You'll notice that the morning after just one heavy night of booze, your skin is dehydrated. This is because alcohol has reduced the hormone that encourages the kidneys to absorb water. Free radicals will also be on the loose, damaging skin cells and causing inflammation, which is why we wake up with puffy eyes and faces as well.

Heavy drinking over a long period can make male and female sexual organs smaller, as well as interfering with normal sexual functions, with results such as the loss of libido in men and the failure to ovulate in women.

Alcohol can inflame the stomach lining and irritate an existing ulcer. Alcohol addicts will have problems with the stomach and oesophagus as a result of frequent vomiting. They might suffer certain forms of dementia, and damage to the nervous system in their arms and legs.

Alcohol's eating away of the body's vitamin B1 (thiamine) supply can result in other types of brain damage over the long term. The short-term effects on the brain, sometimes even for moderate drinkers, we are all too familiar with, and we are probably groaning with embarrassment right now just thinking about it. I will be reminding you of these later in the chapter.

Alcohol disrupts our sleeping patterns and reduces

the quality of what sleep we do get. Alcohol-induced sleep is not REM (Rapid Eye Movement) sleep, the sort we need to have to be fully rested.

Alcohol is a depressant. If it makes us feel stimulated or reckless, it is because it slows down the transmission of brain-cell signals, thereby switching off some of our inhibitions. In this condition, termed the small-assembly neuron world, we can become fearless, aggressive and clumsy.

Finally, if you haven't already reached your horror-story limit, alcohol is responsible for about 3 per cent of cancers, particularly in the mouth, larynx, pharynx and oesophagus. There are links between alcohol and breast cancer too. Cancer of the liver, stomach and colon are also associated with heavy drinking.

The upside of alcohol

The good news. The alcohol in wine can affect our brain in positive ways. It can lift our mood and help relieve stress, that increasing problem in today's traffic-jammed, eat-on-the-run society. Moderate consumers of wine have been shown to have more balanced moods than those who never partake and those who overindulge.

In moderation, the alcohol in wine lowers 'bad' cholesterol, thereby reducing fatty deposits in our blood vessels, and raises levels of 'good' cholesterol (HDL), which itself works to get rid of 'bad' cholesterol. Alcohol in wine acts as an anticoagulant (anti-blood clotting), thinning the blood and helping prevent vascular diseases such as strokes, heart attacks, deep vein thrombosis, oesteoporosis and kidney failure. It has also been found, in moderation, to improve brain function by increasing blood circulation and improving oxygen supplies, thus helping to prevent dementia.

Alcohol as wine is usually consumed at regular intervals and slowly during meals, rather than on its own, sporadically and at varying paces – the way beer and spirits are more often drunk. In theory it can therefore offer the body a gradual protective dose of alcohol, and often at precisely the same time the drinker is eating potentially dangerous saturated fats.

The case for red wine

Research suggesting certain healthy advantages to drinking wine was being carried out around the world at the beginning of the previous century, but some findings have only been brought to light recently. America's early-twentieth-century prohibition of alcohol no doubt played a part in keeping wine's benefits from public attention. Even today in the States are the distinct remains of a highly censorious approach to alcohol consumption. Findings have also been censored in this country in an effort to prevent any increase in alcohol abuse. Our anti-alcohol lobby has been known to discourage health organizations from funding research into the beneficial effects of wine. In winemaking France and Italy, on the other hand, where wine drinking is a daily activity, health professionals have been much more keen to encourage the notion that regular consumption of wine could help prevent heart disease.

It was as recently as 1991 that the correlation between wine consumption and lower instances of heart disease hit the media and the 'French paradox' was born. The result of research carried out by Frenchman Professor Serge Renaud was announced on a CBS news programme. He had discovered that the French suffered much less from cardiovascular diseases than the British and Americans, although they ate a diet just as high in fat. The key factor making the difference seemed to be that the French regularly drank moderate amounts of red wine with their meals.

Red wine mania struck immediately, of course,

particularly among Americans who starting buying it in a frenzy even though many had never even tried it before. At that stage it was not known why red wine had this effect. Further studies in San Francisco in 1994 revealed the presence of antioxidants, and later scientists in London discovered how these antioxidants obstructed the production of endothelin-1 (the 'bad' cholesterol).

The antioxidants in wine derive from the tannins in grapeskins and seeds, hence the red wine mania (but see below for the benefits of white). Antioxidants are found in the form of phenolic bioflavoid compounds (polyphenols), of which the most common types, resveratrol, quercetin, catechin and proanthocyanidins, are five times stronger than vitamin E, the benchmark antioxidant. These potent compounds reach their highest antioxidant effect after two glasses of red wine, inhibiting the process of oxidation which causes the thickening of 'bad' cholesterol in the bloodstream. Thus antioxidants help to prevent the furring up of arteries and consequently help prevent heart disease and stroke – one of the largest disease groups and among the commonest causes of death.

Polyphenols also protect us from free radicals: waste products also resulting from alcohol consumption, among other things, which cause oxidative damage (ageing) and inflammation as well as some cancers. The antioxidant catechin in particular has been identified as an anti-cancer agent. Polyphenols can reduce the risk of developing certain neurodegenerative diseases, such as Alzheimer's and Parkinson's, and reduce insulin resistance, thus helping diabetics. More recent findings suggest that polyphenols may have properties that are beneficial in the case of AIDS, but this is still very much in the research stage.

The discovery that these phenolic compounds can help prevent ageing has naturally been of great interest to beauty product manufacturers (and me). Wine treatments and grapeskin creams, containing antioxidants that claim to work at holding back the wrinkles five times faster than good ol' vitamin E, are now all the rage. You can indulge yourself Hollywood-style and join the likes of Jennifer Aniston being wrapped up, rolled around and rubbed down in grapeskins at Vinothérapie in Bordeaux at Château Smith Haut–Lafite. Visit their website at www.caudalie.com for information on treatments and creams. Their range of products is available worldwide and has developed a cult following. I find, sadly, that few anti-wrinkle creams seem able to prevent the passage of time showing on my face.

Recent findings in Sardinia suggest that wine made from grapes grown at high altitudes is best of all at preventing heart disease. In their elevated position the grapes get more ultra-violet light, which stimulates the production of the polythenol proanthocyanidin. Levels of this are found to be higher in younger wines from warmer climates. Others findings claim that beneficial polyphenol resveratrol is found in greater concentration in cool-climate grapes such as Pinot Noir, which produce it to fight off fungal disease.

And the case for white wine

Polyphenols were not thought to be present in white wine because they come principally from the skins and seeds of grapes – used in the fermentation of red wine to provide colour and flavour but removed before the fermentation of white. Red wine took the stage in the health-benefit show, and a group of Israeli scientists began collaborating to make a white wine with levels of antioxidants to match those of red by extracting polyphenols before removing the skins. Meanwhile, in 2001 research carried out by a German-Italian team showed that white wine has its own antioxidants: tyrosol and caffeic acid, which have significant effects on the oxidation and inflammation within the body caused by free radicals. Moderate consumption, it was suggested, could help protect the body against cancer, osteoporosis and rheumatoid arthritis. The antioxidants in white wine were found to work even more effectively than those in red wine because the molecules were smaller and could get further into the body tissues.

So, who wins the 'battle of the phenols' – red or white wine? Both have their merits, it would seem.

Cardiovascular confusion

Arguments have also been presented to contradict the cardiovascular-benefits story, saying that moderate consumption of alcohol, as protection against heart disease, is only relevant if you are in a high-risk category, namely a man over forty or a post-menopausal woman. If not, then you get no cardiovascular benefits from drinking wine. Indeed, if you drink more than moderate amounts, you are increasing the risk of high blood pressure and thus heart disease and strokes. Others argue that the groundwork that puts you at risk when you are older is being laid by 'bad' cholesterol as early as your twenties, and thus it is not too early to begin moderate consumption as a preventative measure in your twenties.

An argument against the French paradox suggests that the French diet has only recently included a great deal of fatty food, so that it is too early to tell whether French people's health is really being helped by their drinking habits. Dr Renaud himself, twelve years after bringing to life the French paradox, has retreated somewhat, saying it is an 'inexplicable fact' that there is a lower mortality rate from heart-related illness in France than other countries. It looks to me like we are not much clearer about what's happening than we were in the first place.

Sex differences

What is clear is that drinking alcohol is a very different exercise for women than it is for men, and I am sorry to say that women have drawn the shorter straw. Nearly every organ in a woman's body is more vulnerable to alcohol than that in a man's body. We have more fat and less diluting water in our bodies than men, which means a higher concentration of alcohol in our body tissues. Thanks to our different metabolisms, it takes us longer to break down alcohol and sober up. Men have more of the enzyme alcohol dehydrogenase, used by the body to break down alcohol, and some of their supply is found in the stomach. Our much smaller amount does its work later in the metabolic process, in the liver and small intestine. So men start metabolizing earlier and faster, before the alcohol goes into the bloodstream, giving them a great advantage.

Europeans of both sexes have higher levels of alcohol dehydrogenase than Asians, which means most Asians get red faces and fall over more quickly than most Europeans. Europeans have their history to thank for this. While the nomadic Chinese, for example, got off their behinds and set off looking for fresh water when they needed it, Europeans tended to sit around drinking alcohol when the water supplies were not good enough. European metabolisms gradually evolved to handle booze better: women less well than men, however.

Not only do women metabolize alcohol less well than men, we also become addicted to it sooner and experience medical repercussions more quickly. Women who consume two or three drinks daily are at risk of liver cirrhosis – about half the threshold for men, because our livers are doing more, harder work than men's. Even drinking just two glasses a day increases a woman's chances of developing osteoporosis. It just isn't fair.

This is why men and women have different 'sensible drinking' allowances. What exactly the levels should be is, again, a source of debate and confusion. The limit used to be 21 units a week for men, and 14 for women. A unit equates to one small glass of wine, half a pint of beer or a standard pub measure of spirits or fortified wines. Under the previous government, the Department of Health guidelines changed to daily instead of weekly limits, on the grounds that drinking in binges posed a more serious risk to health than drinking regular, small amounts. The sensible drinking guidelines were re-set at 3–4 units a day for men and 2–3 for women, with at least one alcohol-free day a week recommended. This has been widely – and wrongly – interpreted as an increase of the recommended limit to 28 units a week for men and 21 units a week for women.

Safest is to remember that sensible consumption for us, the fairer, fattier, more dehydrated sex, is two to three small glasses of wine a day, with the mandatory minimum of one day off a week. You may not be surprised to hear that 1 in 7 women drink more than this amount.

Drinking wine affects us women differently at different stages. It's important to have all the facts about how alcohol can affect us at crucial times in our lives. And it's not all bad news for us.

Sex

When it comes to sex, men come away worse off than women. A few alcoholic drinks may initially increase a man's desire and make him think he's Don Juan and the girls around him are supermodels, but a few more and his testosterone levels drop faster than his trousers, rendering him more interested in drinking songs and quite unable to perform in the bedroom. For women, on the other hand, alcohol quickly raises our testosterone levels, increasing our libido and making us tigresses in the sack. This effect is heightened for women on the pill, and heightened for non-pill users when they are ovulating. On the other hand, alcohol's effects on the brain can lead us into error of judgement: be careful you don't regret your bedroom bravado the next day. Drink much too much, though, and the will will be gone, even in a woman.

Menstruation

Pliny the Elder might have had an interesting thing or two to say on the subject of wine and health, but when it came to menstruation he clearly lacked understanding. 'On the approach of a woman in this state, wine will become sour, seeds which are retouched by her will become sterile, grafts wither away, garden plants are parched up and the fruit will fall from the tree beneath which she sits.' Thankfully we've come a long way in our thinking since then. It sounds to me like his wife was suffering from a nasty case of dysmenorrhea – period pain, affecting about half of all women these days. If she was, a glass of wine might have helped ease her discomfort. Doctors have found that alcohol helps slow down the uterine contractions that cause pelvic pain during a period. Recent findings at the SUNY Downstate Medical Center in New York suggest a glass of wine might help in the case of PMS as well. Levels of our feel-good hormone slump before a period, but a little alcohol can replenish them. It's a bad time to overdo the drinking, however, as we are at most risk of becoming alcohol-dependent at this time, and it would be unwise to mask the symptoms of PMS long-term, making it harder to understand and monitor the condition.

Further findings suggest that we metabolize alcohol faster mid-cycle. On the other hand, the pill can slow down the metabolism of alcohol, making us drunker for longer.

Fertility

Alcohol may get us in the mood for loving, but it is distinctly less helpful if we are trying to conceive. Drinking even moderate amounts of alcohol can suppress ovulation. Heavy drinking keeps oestrogen levels abnormally high, messing up the reproductive cycle. Ten days' abstinence is recommended before you attempt to conceive. You'll have to rely on oysters and ginger instead.

Pregnancy

For most pregnant women alcohol is the last thing in the world they feel like. They'd much rather eat a chocolate and anchovy sandwich. As to the effects of drinking on the foetus, a verdict has not yet been reached. It has been suggested that a drink a day throughout pregnancy can cause growth defects. Children of mothers who drank throughout pregnancy, particularly in the crucial first three months, tend to be born smaller and have smaller brains, and to achieve less well at school. Other reports have suggested that one or two units of wine, once or twice a week, is not likely to do any harm to the growing foetus. If you do have a thirst for wine during this time, listen to your body and be sensible, but keep amounts very very low, and avoid it altogether in the first three months.

Drink heavily and you run the risk of miscarrying, delivering a very underweight baby or giving birth to a child with FAS – Foetal Alcohol Syndrome, which means growth deficiencies, abnormal joints, poor coordination and short-term memory, and facial malformations. Alcohol crosses the placenta very easily. Even drinking at normal 'sensible' levels (2 or 3 units a day) has been found to increase the risk of spontaneous abortion because alcohol suppresses progesterone, an important hormone in pregnancy.

The damage that might be done to a baby is likely to occur in the first three months when complex organs and the nervous system are being formed. Publicans or restaurateurs who refuse to serve pregnant women (as they often do in America where they live in constant fear of being sued) only know to do so because they see an obvious bump. Abstaining from alcohol at this late stage is less effective.

It is worth bearing in mind that constant worrying about the baby is possibly more harmful than relaxing with the occasional, twice weekly say, glass of wine.

Breastfeeding

Alcohol will be secreted in your breast milk. The odd glass and you might find you have a drowsy baby in your arms (which could be a blessing). Any more and you could slow down the motor development of your child. Heavy drinkers put their baby in serious danger as alcohol's anticoagulant effect can, at worst, cause it to suffer from internal bleeding.

Be aware that the alcohol in a glass of wine will peak in your breast milk about an hour after you drank it; ninety minutes if you drank the wine with a meal. Something to consider when planning a feed.

Breast Cancer

This is a sensitive and worrying subject for many women, particularly if they have a family history of the disease, when they might be increasingly vulnerable to the effects of alcohol. As with many health issues, there is continued controversy. Drinking alcohol increases levels of oestrogen in the body, and oestrogen can promote tumours. Studies have shown an increased risk of developing breast cancer among older women who drink regularly, and an even greater risk for those also using HRT (hormone replacement therapy). Studies have also shown that red wine consumed in moderation can have a protective effect on pre-menopausal women, thanks to the antioxidant resveratrol. Vascular disease kills more women than breast cancer and moderate drinking can help prevent this too. Harvard research has shown that taking 5mg of folate a day can help reduce the risk of breast cancer.

Menopause

There is good news for the menopausal. You have now started to metabolize alcohol in a more masculine way, with your stomach producing more alcohol dehydrogenase. If you have a family history of heart disease, your risk of developing heart problems has increased on reaching menopause, so the cardiovascular benefits of the antioxidants in red wine, combined with your increased tolerance, would seem to be a good enough reason to drink a little wine each day.

Weight

A glass of wine is a fat-free and cholesterol-free source of carbohydrate, but it's got the same calories as a heaped teaspoon of mayonnaise (about 100). Alcohol itself is the second most calorific thing we consume at 7 calories per gram, behind fat at 9 calories/gram and ahead of protein and carbohydrates at 4 calories/gram.

On a night of heavy drinking you are taking in a steady infusion of carbohydrates: 'empty' calories, in fact, which provide energy but not much else. Your body gets used to processing these and adjusts your blood sugar levels to cope. When you stop drinking your body continues processing for a while (it's a bit slow to catch on), so your blood sugar levels drop to low. This makes you crave high-calorie fatty foods, which in other instances you might sensibly avoid. Do you, like me, scream for chocolate, cheese and thickly buttered toast the morning after you've had a few?

Wine drinkers are particularly badly off in this respect, I am sorry to say, because we so often combine our vinous pleasure with feasting. More than this, wine actually gets our gastric juices going. Mouth-watering acidity makes us dribble while our tummies rumble. And the riper the grapes used to make the wine, the higher the sugar content. This can either stay as sugar in dessert wine or be fermented out to alcohol in the rest. Either way, we are talking calories: calories in the alcohol, and calories in the rich food we are tempted to eat when our appetites are stimulated and our self-discipline simultaneously weakened.

If calories are a concern for you, stretch drinks out by adding soda water. With a white wine spritzer you'll have fewer calories, less alcohol – and your dignity intact. Or drink lower-alcohol dry wines: the lower the alcohol percentage, the fewer the calories.

People who drink very heavily, however, often lose their appetites altogether, getting from the alcohol enough energy on which to survive and losing interest in proper food altogether: a real health-killer.

What is confusing, however, is that comparative studies of the weight of drinkers and non-drinkers show that boozers don't necessarily pile on the pounds. It seems to be a rule straight from the School of Unfair. If you are overweight in the first place, you are more likely to put on weight by drinking, while thinner people appear not to put weight on when they drink. However, we are all notoriously dishonest (even with ourselves) about how much we eat and drink.

So why not take the alcohol out of the wine? Well, besides being occasionally responsible for behaviour you would rather forget, alcohol adds texture, richness and character. Take this away and you are left with a weedy imitation. I would recommend drinking tastier fruit juice or a soft drink instead.

Allergies

Wine is made up of hundreds of complex chemical compounds and contains certain additives. Unsurprisingly, not all of these agree with all of us.

Sulphur dioxide is used in all winemaking (though less in organic winemaking) as a preservative. It can irritate and encourage allergic reactions, such as asthma, migraines and skin rashes, in certain sensitive types.

Histamines and tannins, prevalent in red wine, can also upset those with allergic tendencies. The flushed cheeks and red-neck syndrome, appearing after a single glass, is a curse many women could do without. Older red wines are better suited to sufferers of this complaint because histamines and tannins become less irritant over time.

Many women prefer to drink white wine instead. On the other hand, the acidity in white and sparkling wine can be unforgiving on a sensitive stomach.

Organic red wine still contains histamines and tannins but should be made using less sulphur dioxide. It is worth trying if you have gone red-faced once too often, or had trouble with headaches or, worse still, with breathing.

Champagne and fizzy wine go to your head more quickly than still wine, perhaps because the carbon dioxide in the bubbles speeds up the alcohol's passage through the stomach and into the intestines, where it is absorbed into the bloodstream and sent on up to your waiting brain. Another argument is that this is more a psychological than physical phenomenon, because fizzy wine is drunk on special occasions when you are already in an overexcitable, celebratory, hyper-receptive mood.

The Brain: A Profile of Little Miss Drunktoomuch

We've all been there. It began with laughter, sped through singing and dancing (badly) on tables, pulled up short at tears (or worse, vomiting) and returned to haunt us with embarrassment. But what was happening to our brain?

The first drink provides stimulation. At this stage Little Miss Drunktoomuch's blood alcohol levels are still fairly low but increased metabolism in the areas of her brain associated with movement are making her more animated. She likes the feelings created by this low dose of alcohol, so naturally she goes on to help herself to more. After three drinks she feels flushed and euphoric.

Her alpha brain waves have increased by now – a sign of being fully relaxed. More blood is flowing to the front of her brain, heightening her mood. This is where she peaks, however. The ride starts going downhill from here. At four drinks, her blood is awash with alcohol and the receptors in her brain, initially activated by the alcohol, are now failing to respond. Her activity levels are dulled, almost as though she has been sedated. By the end of her fifth drink, speaking becomes a challenge and standing far too much of an effort. Her brain is not consuming as much glucose in this state as it should do, especially in the areas where it is needed to help her see straight, and in her cerebellum where movement, speech and memory are controlled. Little Miss Drunktoomuch is feeling groggy. At this point her brain receptors could have made her feel either aggressive or sleepy. Fortunately for our boozing buddy, they do the latter. She slumps in a chair in the corner and goes to sleep. The sleep she is to get now and later tonight is unfortunately not to be restorative. No REM for her. What's more, the next day she doesn't remember much of the evening's final events – such as being carried home like a sack of potatoes having thrown up all over her date's new shirt. And the same system in her brain that causes her sleepiness also affects her memory centre. She is probably not suitably embarrassed *not* to do it again. Only a cranium-aching, stomach-wrenching hangover is likely to put her off repeated overindulgence.

The Hangover

Your mouth feels like it has been sucked dry by a dentist's saliva hoover and your head feels like it has been run over by a steam train. Your tummy feels like it is digesting something deadly poisonous and you can't remember how you got home. Sound familiar?

A hangover is likely if five or more units are consumed over a one- to two-hour period. Of course, this also depends more specifically on your metabolic make-up and your size. Red wine is more likely to give you a hangover than white because it contains more congeners (impurities in alcoholic drinks that give them flavour; prevalent in darker drinks).

Alcohol is a diuretic, causing the kidneys to lose water in urine. When we drink too much alcohol we quickly become dehydrated, losing water-soluble vitamin C at the same time. The body, in desperation, borrows water from other parts of the body, including the brain, which shrinks as a result. Hence the raging thirst, dry tongue and headache the morning after, and why we should always drink water alongside alcohol.

Dehydration also causes us to lose essential elements, such as potassium and sodium, which are key in the functioning of nerves and muscles. Nausea, fatigue and headaches are the result of this as well.

Low blood sugar levels (hypoglycemia) the next day, provoked by the overzealous calorie processing of the night before, can make us weak and tired too – particularly as our sleep was not restorative. Muscles may ache more and you could get cramp if you try an overly energetic session at the gym. If you want to exercise, make sure you are drinking even more water than usual.

Interestingly, the mood changes in women induced by too much alcohol are similar to those observed with PMS.

Hangover Prevention and Cure

A topic rich in mythology and folklore, for which the only real magic solution is moderation or, worse, abstention.

It is always advisable to **eat before** you go out drinking. Food helps slow down the rate at which your body absorbs alcohol, allowing it time to produce the enzymes it needs. You won't get drunk so quickly and you are less likely to want to roll over and die the next day. The best things to eat beforehand are high-fibre carbohydrates, such as baked potatoes, beans and pasta. The glucose released by eating these will also provide you with vital arm-raising and elbow-bending energy for the night ahead.

Drinking plenty of **water** before, during and after an alcohol experience is vital to prevent dehydration and reduce the symptoms of a hangover.

The old student trick of drinking a pint of **milk** before a night out on the tiles has some value. Milk coats the stomach lining with fat, reducing the rate at which the body absorbs alcohol.

Carrot juice is a natural remedy for purging your body of the toxins produced by the breakdown of alcohol. Drink occasionally for a few days after a night of alcohol punishment.

Milk thistle is a herbal remedy that works in much the same way as carrot juice, most importantly in helping to regenerate damaged liver cells. **Extract of globe artichoke** is another liver reviver. It stimulates the production of bile, which can relieve the symptoms of nausea and other tummy trouble. Both of these can be found in health food stores.

Painkillers are not recommended before you go to bed. They mix with the alcohol, and anyway they wear off while you sleep so you won't feel much better by the time you wake up. In the morning they can help with headaches but less so with nausea. **Aspirin** and **ibruprofen** are better than paracetamol, which, according to the US Food and Drug Administration, can increase the damage alcohol does to your liver.

For nausea and headaches, remedies such as **Alka Seltzer** and **Resolve** can help. They contain painkillers (for your head) and bicarbonate (for your tummy).

NAC (**N-acteyl-cysteine**) is an amino-acid supplement found in health stores. It can soak up the destructive chemicals built up in the liver as the poor organ struggles to break down alcohol. NAC contains **cysteine**, an amino acid also found in eggs – and indeed omelettes, fried eggs and prairie oysters all help in the battle against the hangover monster.

Prairie Oyster

If your stomach is up to it, this really does work. In a glass, mix together 1 tsp Worcestershire Sauce, 2 tsp tomato ketchup, 2 dashes lemon juice, 2 dashes olive oil and a pinch of salt and paprika. Slide in an egg yolk, and finish with a little ground pepper. Down in one.

Other Remedies

* **Intox RX** combines NAC with kudzu (a herb that helps reduce alcohol cravings and eliminate hangover symptoms). It also contains valuable vitamins and milk thistle. It comes in capsule form, and you are advised to take two a couple of hours before the party kicks off, and two the morning after. Available from the Nutricentre on 020 7436 0422.
* **Miam!** is the UK equivalent of the Spanish hangover cure, *horchata de chufa*, a chilled milky drink drunk during fiestas to help the Spanish cope with all the overexcitement. Made from the juice that comes from the root of the *Cyperus esculentus* plant, it tastes a bit like you would imagine cactus juice to taste. See www.miam.co.uk to try some.
* **Sports drinks** before bed can help raise depleted levels of potassium and sodium.
* A **banana** in the morning can help replace lost potassium as well as restoring blood sugar levels to near normal.
* **Exercise**, if you are up to it, is a way to detoxify. And to take your mind off how bad you feel and how many friends you've lost.
* A cup of soothing **lemon or ginger tea**, or warm water with grated fresh root ginger, can offer your tummy TLC the morning after.

* Finally, the old faithful: hair of the dog – effective but ill-advised. Although it may pick you up for a while the morning after, the relief it offers is temporary. If you have drunk cheap red wine, it will get the liver working again on the ethanol (broken down first) and leave the methanol (the worse symptom provider) for later. This only prolongs the inevitable agony, and, more worryingly, increases the risk of addiction.

Finally

Look after your hard-working liver in the first place and it will be less likely to let you down. Eat masses of fresh fruit and vegetables – great sources of antioxidants and fibre, which help keep the liver healthy and clean, while replacing lost vitamin C.

And in case this chapter has been enough to put you off ever picking up a glass of alcoholic grape juice again, here is a thought to leave you with. Research in Denmark has shown that wine drinkers have a significantly higher IQ than beer drinkers. They are also better off in terms of personality, psychiatric symptoms and health-related behaviour. I'll drink my glass of wine to that.

CHAPTER ELEVEN

A World of Wine

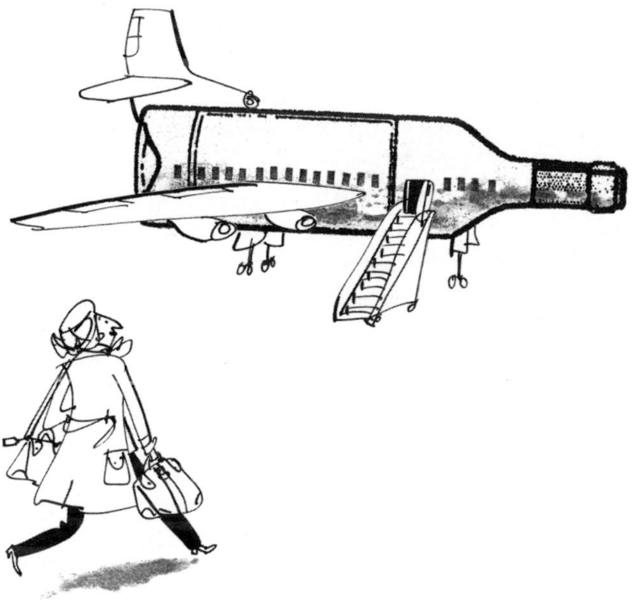

BY NOW, I HOPE, YOU ARE STEEPED IN KNOWLEDGE AND HEADY with enthusiasm. It's time to take one more glorious gulp. I bring you an all-star cast of twenty-first-century wine: where in the world wine is made, what makes each contributing country so extraordinary, and how the future might unfold. You may see more of some stars than others here, and you might even feel some are missing altogether. My commentary relates to how brightly each one is glowing at the moment, which, as with all matters of the cosmos, is subject to constant flux and change. Have your waffle guide in tow and your list of style favourites to hand as we begin a tour of the bright lights in the vinous stratosphere.

Argentina

Argentina is unarguably capable of making some great wines, though the phenomenon is fairly recent. Up until the early 1990s, little worth bothering with was to be found in the country itself (although they produced vast amounts) and none in the UK at all. Improvements in the vineyards and in winemaking practices have made the difference here, just as they did for their Andean next-door neighbour Chile. However, the country's economic crisis at the start of the new millennium inevitably affected the wine industry and sales dropped considerably. A bumper harvest in 2002 gave the winemakers a much-needed boost and hopes are high that the situation will stabilize. Seventy per cent of all production comes out of the region of Mendoza, valued for its high-altitude planting slopes. The beef-dominated diet demands that more, better red grapes are grown than white. Malbec is their red pride and joy, working much better here than in its homeland of south-west France. Torrontes, their own white, makes aromatic, flower-scented wines at inexpensive prices.

Australia

It would have been hard to avoid the wines of Australia as they came hurtling towards our marketplace about ten years ago, making quite a scene. The offer of flavour-packed user-friendliness was too tempting for even some of the most stalwart Europhiles to resist. The Australians were trying out a ground-breaking concept, permissible because they were not restricted by Old World labelling laws: making wine using grapes from as many areas as they liked and blending them together for a consistent result. This way they didn't have to rely on one particular region always offering grapes that were up to scratch. Vintage differentiation was no longer such a concern. But critics have said that many of their wines lack individuality or interest, tasting manufactured rather than distinctive or representative of their origins. Whatever your take on it, the wines, dominated by big brands, are still selling like hot cakes in the UK, giving the long-standing leader, France, something to sweat about, not least thanks to Australia's upfront and well-funded marketing campaigns. Ironically, a more recent problem for the Aussies has been overproduction, resulting in a surplus of wine – even in the UK we can't drink it fast enough. This has led to overzealous discounting in retail outlets: a move that risks cheapening the image of Australian wine in the long term.

Across most of that vast, arid land expanse it's too hot and dry to breathe, let alone make wine, so wine-making areas are mostly restricted to the coast. Having said this, irrigation makes unlikely places workable, such as MIA (Murrumbidgee Irrigation Area). You can find just about any grape variety you could wish for, either succeeding or being toyed with, as well as fruity Traditional Method bubbly and sinful sweet wines, but the chart-toppers across the board are Chardonnay and Shiraz. Big, rich, ripe, unashamedly oaky and alcoholic, these are wines with muscles.

Austria

The home of snow-capped mountains, opera houses and one of the finest crystal manufacturers in the world (Riedel), Austria makes some delicious wines as well. White and sweet wines are their forte, in grape choice and flavour reminiscent of Alsace and Germany but with their own uniquely dear pricing practices: on most occasions worth every mouth-watering penny. Production levels are tiny in global terms; these are hand-crafted wines that revived in quality to a dramatic extent after the additive scandals of the 1980s. Like their vinous cohorts Alsace and Germany, they prefer to allow their aromatic varieties to express their own beguiling charm without too much oak intervention. Styles are defined and labelled by their sweetness levels, just as they are in Germany (see pages 123–4). Their natural, steely acidity means they can age and age and age.

Brazil

Brazil is South America's third biggest producer of wine. In quality terms, their ranking is not so high, which is why we don't see any in the UK at the moment.

Investment and subsequent improvement of winery conditions, as well as a better understanding of how to handle the country's humidity, would make the Brazilians quality contributors in the future.

Bulgaria

Mass production for export – this might sound like a criticism of Bulgarian wines but they are indisputably capable of offering value for money. This is some of the cheapest wine available in the UK. Cabernet Sauvignon is their party trick, and works for value almost every time, while Merlot and Chardonnay have more recently been added to their repertoire. Bulgaria still has an image problem, but increased investments and better marketing management in the next few years might make us think again.

Canada

If you have ever tasted Canadian ice wine, you will remember it. This seductively syrupy substance will leave you drooling for days. Made from super-ripe grapes that have frozen on the vine, the winemaker squeezes out all the sugary sweetness with none of the diluting effect of water. The result is an intense injection of sweet dried fruit with tongue-teasing, give-me-more acidity. Canada is the biggest producer of this particular indulgence, but demand is understandably high and quantities remain small. We should count ourselves lucky to find it in the UK at all: until recently it was banned by the EU. Austria and Germany also make this style of wine: *Eiswein*. Canada's industry as a whole is very new, one of the latest additions to the New World family. Their dry red and white wines are American in influence (ripe and oaky) and priced even further out of reach. Canadians themselves drink much more imported wine than wine of their own making. You are more likely to find their wines in restaurants over here than in wine shops.

Chile

Things are looking pretty hot for Chile at the moment. The country's economy is more stable than its neighbour across the Andes, Argentina, and its share of the market in the UK is on the up and up. The Chileans' secret is an ideal climate (endless sunshine, very little grape rot, shelter from the Andes and freedom from the fatal vine pest, phylloxera), allowing them to make wines cost-effectively and offer them to us at prices to keep us happy. If they are missing anything, it is a strong brand image to lead the way. We might buy their wine by the bucketload but we don't often name-drop Chile. In the meantime, the varieties to look for are Cabernet Sauvignon, Chardonnay, Merlot and, most exciting of all, Carmenère – planted and confused with Merlot for many years, now with its own identity and passport to travel overseas, and with results that are rich and rewarding. The future also holds the promise of more organic wines from this skinny country, as their ideal land, soil and weather make this an enviable possibility.

China

I nearly fell off my bar stool when I found out that China has more acres under vine than Australia. So where are the fruits of this labour? Most of what China has she drinks at home. Investment, and an understanding of what varieties work where in a climate that goes to unhelpful extremes, will help the Chinese become real players in the future. Keep an eye out for them.

England

We could make more fuss of our own wine, though admittedly some of it is hard to swallow. We have utterly uncooperative weather and a funny mix of mostly German-origin varieties, ones that I doubt would taste great even in optimum growing conditions. Sparkling wine is our secret weapon. The grapes needed for this *like* it when it's cold and miserable, weather the region of Champagne also often enjoys. Some sparkling wines from England have knocked the spots off the competition in blind tastings, showing all the nutty complexity of the finest Champagnes from France. Definitely worth trying, if you haven't already.

France

Can you say 'la France' without saying 'du vin'? The wines the French produce offer a vast and often bewildering range of varieties and styles. What's more, the best French wines are the finest in the world, with refined yet complex flavours and endless ageing potential. You only have to look at smart restaurant wine lists or visit auction houses to see this for yourself. France is a powerful role model for many other winemaking countries around the world, and yet the French are drinking less wine than they used to, with the young especially being seduced by spirits and 'alcopops'. Their share of the UK wine market (by volume) has also dropped, by 25 per cent in the last ten years, because we have finally woken up to the fact that they are not the only winemaking country in the world, and that their lower-priced wines can often be trampled over by tastier, better-quality alternatives from elsewhere. French resistance can lie in her inherited winemaking skills and traditions. The French have been squeezing grapes and sipping vinous juice since the time of the Romans. But reluctance to move with the times and take on the competition snapping at her heels, mostly from Australia, could leave her high and dry. New attempts to overhaul the country's wine laws, modernize viticultural practices, increase marketing support and accept the fact that the French might not always be right are helping. Watch this space.

I have written about each major winemaking area of France individually.

Alsace

A region that for a long time suffered an identity crisis – was it French or German? When you try the wines, it is not unforgivable to believe that they still don't know. Dressed in fluted bottles to look like German wines but with the unmistakable flavour and alcohol of French, the best wines are made with their principally white and invitingly intense and aromatic 'noble grapes': Riesling, Muscat, Tokay Pinot Gris and Gewürztraminer. Drink them with oriental and spicy foods to satisfy your sybaritic side.

Bordeaux

To make wines that sell for many thousands of pounds a bottle, this south-west coastal region of France must be doing something right. Indeed they are, and have been for an age or two, which is why their wines have reached such breathtakingly reputable bank-account-emptying heights. Remember that they make plenty of more ordinary, affordable Bordeaux *rouge*, and a little *blanc*, as well. The best reds are divided into two distinct, almost always blended styles – on the right bank of the Gironde river are the Merlot-dominant wines of St-Émilion and Pomerol, and on the left, the Cabernet Sauvignon-strong offerings of the Médoc. The French have found the combination of varieties, soils and climate to perform winemaking miracles almost every year, but there is no guarantee that the weather will go their way, hence the concept of the great (or poor) vintage.

Some years the natural powers-that-be dictate better results than others and the wines are valued accordingly. Nowhere else in the world does it matter as much. The biggest need for the future prosperity of this revered region is to try to stop the top wine prices going any further through the roof while making sure the bottom end are worth putting down in the cellar.

Burgundy

A man of the cloth once famously described drinking a glass of top Burgundy as like 'the good Lord sliding down your neck in velvet pants'. I know just what he meant. Burgundy is a wine that you don't just taste, you feel. The top wines from the Côte d'Or, Chardonnay (white) and Pinot Noir (red), have a texture that fills the mouth and slides around the tongue, engaging and seducing every sense. Their flavours can be so steeped in complexity that every time you revisit the glass you find something else to excite you. Burgundy also boasts Beaujolais among its wine success stories – the only red wine recommended for drinking chilled. Light, fruity and undemanding of its imbiber, and at the other end of the value scale to top-class Grand Cru Burgundy, Beaujolais is drunk by the gallon in bistros immediately on release. (It has very little of the skin tannins needed to preserve it.) The top ten *cru* wines from this area are worth taking more time over, however, and the best even survive a good few years' cellaring. Chablis is the region's other frequently talked about tipple. A Chardonnay but without the oak of its neighbouring Bourgogne Blanc, it is defined by its mineral, stony character, a result of the grape's symbiotic affinity with the region's limestone soils.

Champagne

This small region in the north of France is the sole source of the world's most shaken and sprayed sparkling wine, a wine so adored and admired around the globe that many would decide a celebration not worth considering without it. Champagne houses produce a non-vintage (NV) Champagne every year: a blend of juice from a number of years. Only when the weather has looked sufficiently favourably upon this chilly, chalky-soiled region do the producers get light-headed enough to declare a Vintage. Then the juice comes from that year and the bottle is dated. The traditional method by which the wines are made, causing them to ferment a second time to produce bubbles inside the bottle, has been emulated the world over. But Champagne, the name and the excited state of mind, belongs exclusively to the French.

Jura and Savoie

The Alpine region of Savoie produces wine mostly for its skiers to enjoy mid-piste at a mountain café. The whites are light and refreshing; the few reds they make can be thin and toughly tannic. Jura's nutty *vin jaune* (yellow wine), aged in oak casks for six years until fully oxidized, is much like sherry. *Vin de paille*, its dessert wine, is made with air-dried grapes and high in alcohol. The winemaking of both regions is still firmly rooted in tradition.

Languedoc-Roussillon

Think big when you consider this warm, dry haven in the arc of France's western Mediterranean coast. It's the largest single wine-producing area in the world. There's no doubt you will have tried many of its creations in the past, though you might not have known it at the time: bottles from here are often simply labelled 'Vin de Pays d'Oc'. French country wine, *vin de pays*, is what this area is renowned for, until recently also often referred to as 'cheap plonk'. Investment, increased quality concern, and innovation, allowed in an area where EU laws are less confining, mean the latest results provide ripe gobfuls of flavour. Just what is needed to sing in harmony with the herb-scented, tangy tomato and garlic-infused food of the south. Great value prices too. Serious boozy stickies made from Muscat and known as VDN (*Vin Doux Naturel*) come from this part of the world too, as well as Roussillon's speciality, Banyuls, a fortified red wine. Great news at the beginning or end of a meal.

The Loire

A long and winding river, along the banks of which a multitude of different styles of wine are made. From steely, dry Muscadet to sweet, saliva-driving Vouvray, and from silly pink Anjou rosé to chewy, red Chinon, all the jewels of the Loire valley deserve a visit. The chances are you've already supped Sancerre or Pouilly-Fumé, the Loire's success-soaked Sauvignon Blanc – a million miles both in flavour and distance from the also popular New Zealand versions.

Corsica and Provence

Holiday haven and rosé wine country, capable also of producing spicy and characterful reds. They use many of the same southern French varieties as Languedoc-Roussillon as well as their own natives. Bandol is the top spot in both categories – the reds are wild and spicy and the best are long-ageing; the rosés are a mouth-filling experience you might have sipped at only on the beach but worth taking up with again when you get home.

The Rhône

This vinous valley is divided in two. The northern and southern Rhône's contributions are markedly different. Almost all the wines from the north are red, except for the ethereally perfumed Viognier-based white Condrieu, and the only red variety permitted here is Syrah, responsible for such celebrated names as Côte-Rôtie and

Hermitage. The south has thirteen red varieties to choose from, all of which are allowed into its wallet-stretcher Châteauneuf-du-Pape. The volume of both regions (77 per cent in total) is taken up by the workhorse wine and bistro staple Côtes du Rhône. Quality these days ranges from dire to delicious; the guarantee is it will be reasonably priced.

South-west France

An overspill of Bordeaux heading south, this muddled expanse of regions supplies wines to be treasured as well as those best spat out. The grape varieties are similar to those found further south-east. The flavours of the reds, such as those from Cahors and Madiran (of which there is a greater supply), are traditionally deep, dark and teeth-stain tannic. More recently efforts have been made to make them easier to handle. Jurançon is this region's most distinctive white wine, available in both sweet and dry styles. From here you can also find the great French grape spirit Armagnac. Cognac, its soul sister, comes from north of Bordeaux.

Georgia

Thought to be a birthplace of winemaking, this land was not given the freedom to develop nor was it able to afford a competitive wine industry for most of the last century. Since 1991 it has been undergoing a slow revival. Predictions are that one day Georgia will make wine to compete with the rest of the world. Another one to watch.

Germany

What must it feel like to be so misunderstood? German wines are not all limp-flavoured Liebfraumilch, as we have been busy believing for the last ten or twenty years. The best Rieslings are some of the most interesting and long-ageing wines in the world. Perhaps it's no surprise that first-time-tasters retain a certain amount of suspicion when you announce that this tongue-teasingly delicious wine smells rather like petrol. One sniff and it is hard not to be hooked; one taste and a whole new oral experience will have opened up for you that you will not be able to walk away from. (Although walking will be easier after drinking these wines than many others thanks to the gentle alcohol content of less than 10 per cent.) The enchanting mix of delicate, aromatic, floral fruitiness and endless racy acidity makes these wines worth shamelessly getting on your knees and begging for. The older they get, the more this becomes a beguiling honey and petrol-scented smoky mystique.

Greece

It's a shame about Retsina. This unpalatable pine-resin-infused wine was enough to put most people off ever trying Greek again. Yet some incredibly delicious wines are made in Greece, from a whole host of unique and unpronounceable grape varieties. And so they should, when you think that Greece is pretty much where our modern wine culture began. Ancient Greeks worshipped wine as a gift from their god Dionysus, and didn't let a day go past without at least one drunken orgy. These days they also make wines using the classic international favourites, such as Chardonnay and Cabernet Sauvignon. White wine is where their seductive skills lie for me (and 70 per cent of their production): fruity, aromatic, full-flavoured yet refreshing. We just need a few more wine merchants to get excited about them over here.

Hungary

Hard to imagine when you look at the shelves in wine shops today, but Hungary was once one of the most important wine-producing countries in Europe. Forty years of communism in the last century guaranteed we were not to get much of a share of it, and even now we only really know about its wine culture because of the resurgence of its ancient answer to all our hedonistic dreams: the dessert wine Tokaji, an apricot- and marmalade-flavoured injection of the nectar only nature can provide. Hungary has a strong collection of native white grapes producing bargain, fruity and sometimes aromatic wines, too.

India

Wine is not an obvious match for curry, but nevertheless India is getting busier with the vine and has fairly recently attracted French investment. India's Traditional Method bubbly Omar Khayyám has always been worth celebrating with, but the UK is now starting to showcase some of her more serious still wines as well. Keep tabs on this lot; we may see more excitement yet.

Italy

Named Enotria, 'the land of the vine', by the Ancient Greeks, with a history saturated in the tradition of wine-making, Italy has, amazingly, yet to reach her full and outstanding vinous potential. There is still more land to be unveiled as suitable for certain varieties, and new areas of plantings are giving life to original styles and flavours. Her wines are the UK's third most popular import. More famous for red than for white, Italy's Chianti, from Tuscany, has for too many years been the country's trade-mark brand. Chianti may be the staple of Italian restaurants and where the volume sales are, but it is by no means a fair representation of all that the country can provide. Italy is home to other reds of richness and complexity: from soft, ripe, high-alcohol hitters in the south and in Sicily, to the truffle-scented, long-living, earthy treasures of the north, such as Barolo and Barbaresco. It is also now producing increasingly exciting and powerfully perfumed whites. It was not enough to expect to succeed in the export market with a soapy Soave or a peardroppy Pinot Grigio. Today's consumer wants flavour and character in wine to keep up with the herbs, spices and other ingredients across the range of international cuisine. Two white varieties capable of achieving this are the Arneis grape from Roero, and Cortese (as found in Gavi wines), both from Piemonte in the north and both making more frequent appearances on restaurant wine lists in this country. You must try them if you haven't already. Italy also makes some superb sweet wines from Moscato (Muscat) – unbelievably the only grape to make grape-scented wine. Available in fizzy form Asti as well as *dulce* (lusciously sticky), it is dessert decadence in a glass that has to be tried to be believed. Top tip, girls: Asti is one of few wines particularly cosy in a clinch with milk chocolate.

Lebanon

Most people in the UK have heard of only one wine from the Lebanon; civil war has seen to that. Château Musar is lucky enough to have very little competition, making it priced above its potential. Years spent in oak and bottle give it a mature and heady, slightly resinous perfume. Other operations are now emerging to challenge this export monopoly. But continued political unrest nearby means there are no certainties for Lebanon's viticultural future.

Moldova

This French-colonized former Soviet Republic has the potential to be something in the world of wine, with its suitable climate and a pick-and-mix of the international varietals. One to watch as it emerges from years of being stifled.

Morocco

Think of a typical Moroccan meal of tagine and couscous, with herbs, dates and spices, and you can probably imagine the sort of wine the natives must design to go with it, though as home to many non-drinking Muslims much of it is more appreciated overseas. Juicy, fruity reds are Morocco's strength, made largely from hardy, southern French imported varieties such as Grenache, Syrah and Cinsault (the French ruled here until the middle of the twentieth century). Until a vine sunscreen is invented, they will do best sticking to the robust red varieties that can handle the heat. Their rosés and especially whites are less rewarding. The best wines come from cooler, higher altitudes. Investment is needed.

New Zealand

Two little, lush islands in the middle of the Pacific produce a wine that has become the envy of the rest of the winemaking world. Sauvignon Blanc, pungent, perfumed and tantalizingly tropical, stamped New Zealand firmly on the vinous map. Marlborough in the north of the South Island is where the best of it comes from. Cloudy Bay, the standard-bearer, became a cult wine practically overnight. The vineyards, the most southerly in the world, are expanding every day, yet production here is still tiny by global standards – a twelfth of their Antipodean neighbour's. They are now looking to incite Pinot envy by creating Pinot Noir reds, good enough to be their next big thing. Many examples are already seducing us, though critics are concerned New Zealand hasn't quite got what it takes to rival Burgundy. NZ also make great wines with many of the other major-league varieties: Chardonnay, Cabernet Sauvignon, Merlot and Riesling, as well as ripe-tasting 'Champagne-method' fizz.

Portugal

The Portuguese have been getting port right for a long time – they've got the special formula and thanks to legislation they've got the name. But now they are managing to make red table wine of which they should be increasingly proud. The same varieties that go into their port blends are producing serious, spicy, fruity and affordable table wines for export. They just need time, as well as a bit of faith from overseas consumers, to fully establish their worth. In the meantime, port is still the money-spinner in auction houses around the world. As with Champagne, its price is dictated by the weather in any given year, and therefore whether a Vintage can be joyfully declared. Madeira, the fortified wine that comes from their island of the same name, is Christmas in a glass, though we need to realize that's not the only time we can enjoy it. Portugal is also the world's principal supplier of wine corks.

Romania

This Eastern European country has a Latin heart, giving it a leg-up when it comes to wine. On the same latitude as France, its climate for grape-growing is hot and drier and in many ways more reliable. Until now, most of the results of their hard work have been consumed at home, but Romanians might yet be a force to be reckoned with overseas, particularly with their whites (three-quarters of production), and the revival of their historically celebrated, enticingly aromatic dessert wine, Cotnari.

South Africa

Besides being home to some of the most beautiful scenery in the world, South Africa is also proving itself to be a pretty serious place to make wine. Thanks to Mandela, this Rainbow Nation is now free to export its vinous propositions. Since the breakdown of apartheid, investment and advances in technology have meant that these wines have become increasingly worth experiencing. Most of the key international varieties are in on the action, as well as their own spicy red grape invention, Pinotage. The main production areas are centred round the cooler southern Cape, the mountain slopes making the most suitable spots for planting. Stellenbosch is where the majority of what we now enjoy comes from. Bordeaux varieties seem to like it here the most, namely Sauvignon Blanc and Semillon for whites and Cabernet Sauvignon, Cabernet Franc and Merlot for reds, though plenty of Chardonnay and some Syrah, Cinsault and Pinot Noir (in other cooler parts) are planted too. Chenin Blanc (of Vouvray fame in France), or Steen as they call it locally, is responsible for nearly a quarter of all plantings. South Africa's success in the UK market is firming up thanks to the development of increasingly strong brands. If the South Africans can keep up production levels while polishing up consistency and quality, their best-sellers will soon be household names.

Spain

Spain is still undergoing a vinous revolution. A lot of work needed to be done to rebuild a nation of winemakers suffering from over-oaking disease – traditional winemaking practices had them putting red and white wine indiscriminately in large old barrels and forgetting about them for years. Younger, fresher wines are being called for and the Spanish are responding. One of their replies is delicate, flowery-scented, peachy Albariño from the cool, coastal, northern region of Rias Biaxas in Galicia. The Rioja region was the red centre for well over a hundred years (with peaks and troughs), but copycat areas, such as Navarra and Valdepeñas, are now showing similar ability. Ribera del Duero is responsible for some of the country's most serious reds and is home to the cult, worth-committing-crime-for wine Vega Sicilia. Rueda is also one to watch for its improving whites. Spain might have the most land under vine (relatively) in the world but she doesn't produce the most wine – many areas where plantings still exist are harsh and infertile. You'll notice from the relatively limited supplies of their wines on our shop shelves that most of what the Spaniards make they keep for themselves. But Cava, the Spanish answer to Champagne though made with different grape varieties, is one they are more than willing to share. And so they should do: they produce enough of the stuff and they sell it very cheaply. As a result, the Spanish don't use their light, lemony fizz to mark a special occasion – they drink it any time, anywhere, much as they do their Jerez, better known to us as sherry. Sherry is Spain's life water, designed to accompany every delicious tapas-style thing the Spanish eat. This it can do easily since it comes in such an array of contrasting styles, from sit-up-straight dry (Fino) to slither-around-on-the-sofa sticky (Pedro Ximenez), two epicurean extremes in one misunderstood brand name. Please don't knock sherry till you've tried it. More complexity of satisfying flavour for your money than any other libation on the planet.

Switzerland

Besides being the home of snow storms and Swatch watches, Switzerland also makes a certain amount of good wine. Like everything else you touch when you are there, it's expensive, and you probably do have to be there to try it since most of their wine the Swiss keep at home. Whites are better than reds and can be engagingly refreshing. Chasselas is their favourite native white grape; otherwise look for Malvoisie (Pinot Blanc), Pinot Gris and Chardonnay. Like their Alpine bedfellows from Jura and Savoie, these wines are a tired skier's saviour. The reds are best contemplated over a bubbling fondue.

Tunisia

The wines from this other North African country are forgivably mistaken with those of Morocco – warm, rustic and with conserve-sweet ripeness. The French historically had a great influence here (much Tunisian wine was sent to France to pad out poor vintages) and now investors also include Germany and Italy. Affordable-quality supermarket stock.

USA

The States of America are not united when it comes to their ability to make wine, which is why I'm writing individually on the few, significant contributing states.

California

This is where over 90 per cent of all US wines are made and it is home to the UK's number-one-selling brand, Ernest and Julio Gallo. Know it? The rolling hills, the sea breezes and the ceaseless summer sunshine make this an American dream of a location to grow grapes and make wine. Classified as a country of the New World clan, the wine industry here reawoke in the 1960s after years of prohibition and since then has gone from strength to strength. The wines do well in the UK because they are reliable, look good, offer sweet ripe flavour and are clearly labelled with grape varieties. They sell so well at home, however, where people are prepared to pay silly money for them, that their prices over here are inflated. Their average bottle price is the third highest in the UK. Cabernet Sauvignon and Chardonnay are their classic success stories, in demand the world over, while Zinfandel is their more unique conquest – available in anything from the bottom-end, embarrassing 'blush' rosé to the top-end, proud, spicy reds.

Oregon

Cool, hilly Pinot country where the whole family (Pinot Noir, Pinot Gris and Pinot Blanc) are growing up into solid individuals. Temperamental Pinot Noir is Oregon's greatest conquest, brimming with red berry fruit, enough, the winemakers there would have us believe, to unsteady Burgundy. Critics may argue that this oversensitive (at the best of times) variety needs a bit more love and understanding before it can compete. The newer Pinot Gris varieties that are emerging are increasingly full of flavour and aromatic perfume. To be tried.

Washington State

Hot dry plains where red varieties do best. Cabernet Sauvignon and Merlot are the major shareholders, producing reds of incredible density and opulently ripe fruit. As a result of the limited quantities, these wines, and those of Oregon, are more often found in restaurants here than shops.

Uruguay

A winemaking region in South America you don't hear mentioned very often. There's not a lot of this on sale in the UK, which is probably why. The red variety Tannat works for the Uruguayans, softer and more accessible there than in its original home of Madiran in south-west France. Look out for this, as well as the more common varietal names.

What does the future hold?

Where to next? Despite this wealth of wine, this panoply of styles and flavours, the wine world is in many ways homogenizing. Export from countries who used to keep their wine to themselves has increased global competition. Producers around the world are finding successful flavour formulas, adapting different environments and adopting similar techniques to create and then recreate them (such as sweetish, oak-chip-flavoured Chardonnay). The marketeer's role is, worryingly, becoming as important as the winemaker's. The results are brand successes, like Gallo, Jacob's Creek, Kumala and Fat Bastard.

For now, though, each country or region continues to develop at its own pace. Some are more concerned with making flavours to order, and others with making us like what they've got. For the past ten years or so the divide has been between two competing factions: the Old World (Europe) and the New (Australia, New Zealand, South Africa, South America and the United States). The former represents tradition and history, the latter innovation and experimentation. Now the battle lines are becoming blurred, and the roles are being reversed. Much of Europe is making wine the 'modern' way, while the southern hemisphere and the States are borrowing the techniques of the past. Fast and efficient communications and travel potential mean that countries are exchanging and swapping not only varieties and ideas but winemakers too, many of whom are almost permanently in-flight to their next vintage. Fat-cat companies are investing, merging and buying out others across the globe.

Investment, of course, is needed to bring many of the lesser-known, domestic-market-only winemaking industries into the twenty-first century and to dust them down ready to face the competition. This is, however, at the risk of their vinous individuality. The shift from local producer to global is bound to force a change in the content of what is delivered.

What happens next in terms of style depends a great deal on what we, the consumer, choose to buy. Certainly, women increasingly fashion and form the styles and flavours of wine. Predictions are that the UK market by 2005 will be 37 per cent up on 2000, driven largely by the female consumer. The more we think about, talk about, taste and buy wine, the more influence we will have over what is made available to us. Women have gone potty for New World wines, for example, particularly Australia's, for their flavour, quality, perceived consistency and value for money (not to mention creative packaging). How our wines look and what they are called is also in our hands. Wine is increasingly being marketed at us, women, designed to catch our eye on the shelf or stop us in our tracks to look at or listen to an advert. Name, label design, bottle shape and colour, technical information and waffle-rich descriptions are all part of the sell.

Wine will be sealed differently in the future if the problem of 'corked' wine is not solved. Already plastic corks, and screw caps for quick-drinking, young white wines, are filtering through the market. Recent findings suggest that screw caps may be beneficial for wines that are to be aged as well, as oxygen trapped in the neck of the bottle helps mature the wine over time. Only traditionalism and the thrill of the cork 'pop' stands in the way. If caps take over, the cork industry of Portugal will be well and truly screwed.

And what will the hottest varieties be? What will it be cool to be seen with? What varietal buzzwords will A-list drinkers want to name-drop?

As we drink more wine, so we require a greater choice of grape varieties that taste exciting on their own but also complement the many different food flavours we enjoy, varieties with original and tantalizing aromas and palates to reawaken our senses after years of laziness in the land of common or garden Chardonnay.

Viognier was to become the 'new' Chardonnay. Growers started putting down roots all over the globe. So far it hasn't taken off. My feeling is that too many examples, especially from the New World, are bold, brassy and overly alcoholic. You don't just taste it; it hits you. This is quite unlike the more refined yet seductively aromatic Arneis from the northern climes of Italy. Versions from Roero are peachy, fresh and inviting, with both enough weight for food and enough delicacy for drinking alone. This is a wine to fill your fridge with, as is Albariño, the Spaniards' most interesting white and the closest thing they've got to a Riesling, which revels in the rain-riddled climate of Galicia. The fresh, fruity, floral offer it demonstrated in its youth is now showing potential to become something complex and honeyed with age. More than suitable to be served with a myriad of flavours above and beyond Spanish seafood, Albariño also gets my vote as a variety of the future.

On the red side, divination is more complex. There is no single variety in need of replacing because we have tired of it. Yes, clever Cabernet Sauvignon gets everywhere and is planted and drunk by almost everyone, but so too are mellow Merlot and spicy Syrah (Shiraz). My hope is that characterful Carmenère (Merlot's doppelgänger) will continue to prove its worth, even perhaps outside of Chile. I hope too that Carignan, the workhorse grape of the bottom half of France, will further demonstrate its potential beyond blending and rustic country contributions. These are both food reds, rich in colour, fruit and spice. The toughness of tannin they show off in their younger days gives hope for graceful ageing. Finally, Italy's Sangiovese (of Chianti fame) and Spain's Tempranillo (of Rioja) have been spotted holidaying in exotic faraway locations such as Australia and the States. The results so far show real promise, and hopes are they will be unpacking their suitcases and putting down real roots in the future.

Next time you are tempted to spend an evening with Mr Reliable brand – think again. It is true that brands are often a safe option, a glass of certainty and a way into wine for first-time drinkers, their presentation eye-catching and accessible. For the countries concerned, brands are a valuable tool with which to increase consumer awareness. But they are not where excitement, unforgettable experiences or even some of the real bargains lie. For these we need to look, and shop, around. Not all wine is worth drinking, and some of it is so valuable (or overpriced) we are too afraid even to try, but if we have the chance to mould what we drink in the future, why not take this opportunity to diversify, and start now?

I hope this book will have encouraged you to explore and to experiment, to choose wonderful wines to make your night or to mark a memorable occasion, wines you will think and talk about and remember. Wine drinking is a vast and thrilling arena of sensory discovery. Don't let the lads have all the fun.

Hic!

Index